JEAN ANOUILH

The Lark

translated by
CHRISTOPHER FRY

METHUEN DRAMA

A METHUEN MODERN PLAY

First English edition published by Methuen & Co. Ltd., June 2nd, 1955
Reprinted twice
School edition 1959
Paperback edition 1961
Reprinted four times
Reprinted by Eyre Methuen Ltd., 1973
Reprinted four times
Reprinted 1984, 1985 by Methuen London Ltd.
Re-issued in this edition in 1986

Reprinted in 1989 by Methuen Drama,
Michelin House, 81 Fulham Road, London SW3 6RB.

ISBN 0 413 413101

CAUTION

Printed and bound in Great Britain by
Cox & Wyman Ltd, Reading, Berkshire

This play was first presented at The Lyric Theatre, Hammersmith, on May 11th, 1955, with the following cast, in the order of their appearance:

BEAUCHAMP, *Earl of Warwick*	RICHARD JOHNSON
CAUCHON, *Bishop of Beauvais*	LAURENCE NAISMITH
JOAN	DOROTHY TUTIN
HER FATHER	PETER DUGUID
HER MOTHER	ALEXIS FRANCE
HER BROTHER	BARRY MacGREGOR
THE PROMOTER	LEO McKERN
THE INQUISITOR	MICHAEL GOODLIFFE
BROTHER LADVENU	MICHAEL DAVID
ROBERT DE BEAUDRICOURT, *Squire of Vaucouleurs*	DAVID BIRD
BOUDOUSSE, *a guard*	CHURTON FAIRMAN
AGNES SOREL	HAZEL PENWARDEN
THE YOUNG QUEEN	CATHERINE FELLER
CHARLES, *the Dauphin*	DONALD PLEASENCE
QUEEN YOLANDE	LUCIENNE HILL
ARCHBISHOP OF RHEIMS	JOHN GILL
M. DE LA TREMOUILLE	PETER CELLIER
PAGE TO THE DAUPHIN	DAVID SPENSER
CAPTAIN LA HIRE	GEORGE MURCELL
THE HANGMAN	GARETH JONES
AN ENGLISH SOLDIER	NORMAN SCACE

The play directed by PETER BROOK.
Scenery and costumes based on designs by
JEAN-DENIS MALCLÈS

PART ONE

A simple, neutral setting. The stage is empty at first; then the characters enter by twos and threes. The costumes are plain. JOAN *wears man's clothes throughout the play.* WARWICK *is the last to enter.*

WARWICK. Well now; is everyone here? If so, let's have the trial and be done with it. The sooner she is found guilty and burned the better for all concerned.

CAUCHON. But, my lord, before we do that we have the whole story to play: Domremy, the Voices, Vaucouleurs, Chinon, the Coronation.

WARWICK. Theatrical poppycock! You can tell that story to the children: the beautiful white armour, the fluttering standard, the gentle and implacable warrior maid. The statues of her can tell that story, later on, when policies have changed. We might even put up a statue ourselves in London, though I know at the moment that sounds wildly improbable: but you never know, in a few hundred years it might suit His Majesty's Government for some reason or other. But, as for now, I am Beauchamp, Earl of Warwick; and I've got my grubby little witch lying on the straw in the dungeon at Rouen, and a fine packet of trouble she has been, and a pretty sum she has cost us; but the money's been paid, and the next thing is to put her on trial and burn her.

CAUCHON. Not immediately. Before we come to that, there's the whole of her life to go through. It won't take very long, my lord.

WARWICK (*going to a corner resignedly*). Well, if you insist. An Englishman knows how to wait. (*Anxiously.*) I hope you're not expecting me to stand by while you go through that monstrous farce of a coronation again. And all the battles as well—Orleans, Patay, Beaugency?—I may as well tell you now, I should find that in very poor taste.

CAUCHON (*smiling*). Put your mind at rest, my lord. There are too few of us here to stage the battles.

WARWICK. Good.

CAUCHON. Joan.

> *She looks up.*

You may begin.

JOAN. May I begin wherever I like?

CAUCHON. Yes.

JOAN. I like remembering the beginning: at home, in the fields, when I was still a little girl looking after the sheep, the first time I heard the Voices, that is what I like to remember. . . . It is after the evening Angelus. I am very small and my hair is still in pigtails. I am sitting in the field, thinking of nothing at all. God is good and keeps me safe and happy, close to my mother and my father and my brother, in the quiet countryside of Domremy, while the English soldiers are looting and burning villages up and down the land. My big sheep-dog is lying with his head in my lap; and suddenly I feel his body ripple and tremble, and a hand seems to have touched my shoulder, though I know no one has touched me, and the voice says——

SOMEONE IN THE CROWD. Who is going to be the voice?

JOAN. I am, of course. I turned to look. A great light was filling the shadows behind me. The voice was gentle and grave. I had never heard it before, and all it said to me was: "Be a good and sensible child, and go often to church." But I *was* good, and I *did* go to church often, and I showed I was sensible by running away to safety. That was all that happened the first time. And I didn't say anything about it when I got home; but after supper I went back. The moon was rising; it shone on the white sheep; and that was all the light there was. And then came the second time; the bells were ringing for the noonday Angelus. The light came again, in bright sunlight, but brighter than the sun, and that time I saw him.

CAUCHON. You saw whom?

JOAN. A man in a white robe, with two white wings reaching from the sky to the ground. He didn't tell me his name that day, but later on I found out that he was the blessed St. Michael.

WARWICK. Is it absolutely necessary to have her telling these absurdities all over again?

CAUCHON. Absolutely necessary, my lord.

WARWICK *goes back to his corner in silence, and smells the rose he has in his hand.*

JOAN (*in the deep voice of the Archangel*).—Joan, go to the help of the King of France, and give him back his kingdom. (*She replies in her own voice.*) Oh sir, you haven't looked at me; I am only a young peasant girl, not a great captain who can lead an army.—You will go and search out Robert de Beaudricourt, the Governor of Vaucouleurs. He will give you a suit of clothes to dress you like a man, and he will take you to the Dauphin. St. Catherine and St. Margaret will protect you. (*She suddenly drops to the floor sobbing with fear.*) —Please, please pity me, holy sir! I'm a little girl; I'm

3

happy here alone in the fields. I've never had to be responsible for anything, except my sheep. The Kingdom of France is far beyond anything I can do. If you will only look at me you will see I am small, and ignorant. The realm of France is too heavy sir. But the King of France has famous Captains, as strong as you could need and they're used to doing these things. If they lose a battle they sleep as soundly as ever. They simply say the snow or the wind was against them; and they just cross all the dead men off their roll. But I should always remember I had killed them. Please have pity on me! ... No such thing. No pity. He had gone already, and there I was, with France on my shoulders. Not to mention the work on the farm, and father, who wasn't easy.

Her FATHER, *who has been wandering around her* MOTHER, *suddenly speaks.*

FATHER. Where has that girl got to?

MOTHER (*going on with her knitting*). She is out in the fields.

FATHER. Well, I was out in the fields, and I'm back home again. It's six o'clock. She's no business to be out in the fields.

BROTHER. She's sitting under the Fairy Tree, staring at nothing. I saw her when I went to fetch in the bull.

PROMOTER (*from among the crowd*). The Fairy Tree! Note that, gentlemen, if you will. Note the superstition. The beginning of witchcraft already. The Fairy Tree! I ask you to note that!

CAUCHON. There are Fairy Trees all over France, my Lord Promoter. It's in our own interest not to refuse the fairies to these little girls.

PROMOTER (*primly*). We have our saints. That should be sufficient.

4

CAUCHON (*conciliating him*). Later on, certainly. But I mean while they are still very young; as Joan was; not yet fifteen.

PROMOTER. By fifteen they know everything: they're as old as Eve.

CAUCHON. Not Joan: Joan at that time was very simple and innocent. It will be another matter when we come to the trial; I shan't spare her Voices then. But a little girl shall keep her fairies. (*Firmly.*) And these discussions are under my charge.

The PROMOTER *bows, and retires, unmollified.*

FATHER (*bursting out afresh, to the* BROTHER). So that's where you say she is? And what does she think she's doing there, sitting under the tree?

BROTHER. Try and find out! She's just staring in front of her as if she was expecting something. And it isn't the first time either.

FATHER. Well, why didn't you tell me when you saw her before, then? Aren't you old enough to know what trouble there is with girls of her age, you little fool? What do you think she was expecting, eh? Somebody, not something, idiot! She's got a lover, and you know it! Give me my stick!

MOTHER (*gently, still knitting*). You know quite well, Joan's as innocent as a baby.

FATHER. Maybe she is. And girls as innocent as babies can come to you one evening and hold up their faces to be kissed, and the next morning, though you've kept them locked in their room all night, what has happened? You can't see into their eyes at all: they're avoiding you, and lying to you. They're the devil, all at once.

5

PROMOTER (*raising a finger*). The word has been said, my lords, and by her father!

MOTHER. How do you know that? The day I married you I was as innocent as Joan, and I daresay you could look into my eyes just as well next morning.

FATHER (*muttering*). That's nothing to do with it.

MOTHER. Who are these other girls you've known, then, that you've never told me about?

FATHER (*thundering to cover his embarrassment*). I tell you it's got nothing to do with it! We're not talking about other girls, we're talking about Joan! Hand me that stick. I'm going to look for her, and if she's been meeting somebody on the quiet I'll skin them alive!

JOAN (*smiling gently*). I was meeting someone on the quiet, and his solemn voice was saying: " Joan! Joan! What are you waiting for? There's a great sorrow in the realm of France."—" Holy Sir of Heaven, I'm so afraid, I'm only a young village girl; surely you've made a mistake? "—"Does God make mistakes, Joan? " (*She turns to her Judges.*) How could I have answered Yes?

PROMOTER (*shrugging*). You should have made the sign of the cross.

JOAN. I did, and the Archangel made it, too, all the time keeping his eyes carefully on mine, and the church clock sounded.

PROMOTER. You should have cried: Vade retro Satanus!

JOAN. I don't know Latin, my Lord.

PROMOTER. Don't be an idiot! The devil understands French. You should have cried: Get thee behind me, foul Satan, and don't tempt me again.

JOAN. But, my Lord, it was St. Michael.

PROMOTER (*sneering*). So he told you. And you were fool enough to believe him.

JOAN. Yes, I believed him. He couldn't have been the devil. He shone with light; he was beautiful.

PROMOTER (*losing his temper*). So is the devil, so is the devil, I tell you!

JOAN (*scandalised*). Oh, my Lord!

CAUCHON (*calming the* PROMOTER *with a gesture*). These subtle theological points, my lord Promoter, are proper for debating between ourselves, but they're beyond the understanding of this poor girl. No good is served by shocking her.

JOAN (*to the* PROMOTER). You're telling a lie, Canon! I haven't any of your learning, but I know the devil is ugly, and all that's beautiful is the work of God.

PROMOTER (*sneering*). Very charming, simple and stupid! Do you think the devil is stupid? He's a thousand times more intelligent than you and I put together. Do you think when he comes to snare a soul he would come like a horror of the flesh, with black ploughed skin and a snouting tusk like a rhinoceros? If he did, souls would fly to virtue at the sight of him. I tell you he chooses a moonlit summer night, and comes with coaxing hands, with eyes that receive you into them like water that drowns you, with naked women's flesh, transparent, white . . . beautiful——

CAUCHON (*stopping him sternly*). Canon! You are losing your way! This is very far from Joan's devil, if she has seen one. I beg you not to confuse your devil with hers.

PROMOTER (*flushed and confused in front of the smiling crowd*). I beg your pardon, my lord; there is only one devil.

CAUCHON. Go on, Joan.

JOAN (*still troubled*). If the devil is beautiful, how can we know him?

PROMOTER. By asking your parish priest.

JOAN. Can we never know by ourselves?

PROMOTER. No. That is why there is no salvation outside the church.

JOAN. Only rich people have a parish priest always at hand. It's hard for the poor.

PROMOTER. It is hard for everyone to escape damnation.

CAUCHON. My lord Promoter, let her talk with her Voices in peace and quiet. It is the beginning of the story. We mustn't reproach her with them yet.

JOAN (*continuing*). Another time it was St. Catherine and St. Margaret who came to me. (*She turns to the* PROMOTER *with a slightly mischievous defiance.*) They were beautiful, too.

PROMOTER (*blushing, but unable to prevent himself*). Did they appear to you naked?

JOAN (*smiling*). Oh, my lord! Do you imagine that God can't afford clothes for the saints in heaven?

The CROWD *chuckles at this answer, and the* PROMOTER *sits down confused.*

CAUCHON. You see, you make us all smile with your questions, my lord Promoter. Be wise enough to keep your interruptions until we come to the serious heart of this business. And when we do so, particularly when we come to judge her, remember that the soul in this little arrogant body is in our care. Aren't you risking very much confusion in her mind, to suggest to her that good and evil are no more than a question of clothes? It is true certainly, that our saints are traditionally represented as clothed; yet, on the other hand——

8

JOAN (*to the* PROMOTER). Our Lord is naked on the cross.

CAUCHON (*turning to her*). I was going to say so, Joan, if you had not prevented me. It isn't for you to correct the reverend Canon. You forget who you are; you forget that we are your priests, your masters and your judges. Beware of your pride, Joan. If the devil one day wins you for his own, that is the way he will come to you.

JOAN. I know I am proud. But if God didn't mean me to be proud, why did He send an Archangel to see me, and saints with the light of heaven on them to speak to me? Why did He promise I should persuade all the people I have persuaded—men as learned and as wise as you— and say I should ride in white armour, with a bright sword given me by the King, to lead France into battle: and it has been so. He had only to leave me looking after the sheep, and I don't think pride would ever have entered my head.

CAUCHON. Weigh your words, Joan; weigh your thoughts. It is your Saviour you are accusing now.

JOAN (*crossing herself*). God guide me. His will be done, if His will is to make me proud and damned. That is His right, as well.

PROMOTER (*unable to contain himself*). Terrible! What she says is terrible! God's will to damn a soul? And you all listen to this without a murmur, my lords? I see here the seed of a fearful heresy which will one day tear the Church apart.

   The INQUISITOR *has risen. He is an intelligent looking man, spare and hard, speaking with great quietness.*

INQUISITOR. Listen carefully to what I am going to ask you, Joan. Do you think you are in a state of grace at this moment?

9

JOAN (*firmly*). At what moment, my lord? Is it the beginning, when I hear my Voices, or the end, when my King and all my friends have deserted me, when I doubt and recant and the Church receives me again?

INQUISITOR. Don't evade my question. Do you think you are in a state of grace?

All the PRIESTS *are watching her in silence; it seems a dangerous question.*

LADVENU (*rising*). My lord Inquisitor, it is a formidable question for a simple girl who believes in all sincerity that God has called her. I ask that her reply shall not be held against her: she is risking quite unwittingly——

INQUISITOR. Quiet, Brother Ladvenu! I ask what I consider good to ask. Let her answer my question. Do you think you are in a state of grace, Joan?

JOAN. If I am not, may God in His goodness set me there. If I am, may God in His goodness keep me so.

The PRIESTS *murmur. The* INQUISITOR *sits again, inscrutable.*

LADVENU (*quietly*). Well answered, Joan.

PROMOTER (*muttering, annoyed by* JOAN'S *success*). What of it? The devil has cunning, or he wouldn't be the devil. It isn't the first time he has been asked that question. We know what he is; he has his answers all ready.

WARWICK (*bored, to* CAUCHON). No doubt this is all very interesting, my lord, but if you go on at this rate we shall never get to the trial, never have her burnt, never get anywhere. I said she could take us over the old ground again, if you thought it so necessary, but let her get on with it. And let us come to the essentials. His Majesty's Government have to discredit this wretched little Charles Valois, at once; it's imperative that we should let

10

Christendom know that the Coronation was all a humbug, the performance of a witch, a heretic, an army's whore.

CAUCHON. My lord, we're trying her only for heresy.

WARWICK. I know that; but I have to make more of it for the sake of the troops. The findings of your trial, I'm afraid, will be too rarefied for my soldiers. Propaganda, my lord Archbishop, is black or white. The main thing is to say something pretty staggering, and repeat it often enough until you turn it into a truth. It's a new idea, but believe me, it will make its way. The essential thing, so far as I am concerned, is that the girl should be a nonentity, whatever she is in fact. And what she is in fact is of no particular importance to His Majesty's Government. Personally, I must admit, I find the girl attractive. The way she takes the wind out of your sails gives me a lot of pleasure; and her seat on a horse is very good: that's rare in a woman. If the circumstances had been different, and she had belonged to my own set, I should have enjoyed a day's hunting with her. But unfortunately there's been this damned Coronation, and that was nobody's notion but hers in the first place. Really, my lords, what impudence! To have himself crowned King of France right under our noses: a Valois, King of France! and to do it at Rheims, our territory! To dare to pick France out of our pockets, and pilfer the English heritage! Luckily, God is on the side of England, as he satisfactorily proved at Agincourt. God and our right. Two ideas completely synonymous. And moreover, inscribed on our coat-of-arms. So rattle her through the rest of it, and have her burned, and not so much talk. Earlier on I was joking. I give it ten years, and this whole incident will have been forgotten.

CAUCHON (*sighing*). God grant so, my lord.

WARWICK. Where had we got to?

FATHER (*coming forward with his stick*). To where I was going out to find her, sitting under her tree, waiting to get herself into trouble, the little bitch. And I can tell you she'll be sorry she ever began it! (*He drags* JOAN *up by the wrists.*) What are you doing here, eh? Tell me what you're waiting about here for, when you know you ought to be indoors, eating your supper!

JOAN (*stammering, shy at being surprised, raising her arm to protect her face*). I didn't know it was so late. I had lost count of the time.

FATHER. That's it, you lost count of the time! And what else have you lost that you daren't tell me? (*He shakes her abominably.*) Who made you forget it was so late? I heard you as I came along, calling out goodbye to somebody. Well, who was it?

JOAN. St. Michael, father.

FATHER (*giving her a resounding slap on the face*). You make fun at your father, you'll be sorry! I won't have any girl of mine sitting out in the fields waiting for any man who wants to find her. You'll marry the decent fellow we choose for you, or I'll break every bone in your body!

JOAN. I've done nothing wrong, father: truthfully it was the blessed St. Michael who spoke to me.

FATHER. And when you can't hide your sinning any longer, and every day it grows bigger in you for all to see, and you've killed your mother with grief, and your brothers have to join the army to get away from the scandal in the village, it will be the Holy Ghost who brought it on us, I suppose? I'll tell the priest: not content with whoring,

12

you have to blaspheme: and you'll be shut up in a convent on bread and water, my girl.

JOAN (*kneeling before him*). Father, stop shouting, you can't hear what I say. I promise you, by our Saviour, I'm telling you the truth. They've been coming for a long time now to ask things of me. It is always at the mid-day Angelus or the evening Angelus; always when I'm praying, when I am least sinful and nearest to God. Above all doubt, surely it must be true. St. Michael has appeared to me, and St. Margaret, and St. Catherine. They speak to me, and they answer when I question them, and each one says the same as the others.

FATHER (*pulling her about*). Why should St. Michael speak to you, you little idiot? Does he speak to me? Natural enough, if he had something to say to us, he'd say it to me, the head of the family. Does he speak to our priest?

JOAN. Father, as well as shaking me and shouting at me, try to understand what I'm saying. I'm so alone, and they want me to do so much. For three years I've been trying not to believe them, but all that time they've been saying the same thing. These voices I hear: I can't go on fighting them all by myself. I've got to do what they say.

FATHER. The voices you hear? Do you want to drive me mad?

JOAN. They say it can't wait any longer; the time has come when I have to say yes.

FATHER. What can't wait any longer, idiot? What are they telling you to do, what you call these Voices? Voices! Well, it's better than being deaf!

JOAN. They tell me to go and save the realm of France which is in grave danger of being destroyed. Is it true?

13

FATHER. Heavens above! Of course the realm of France is in danger of being destroyed. It isn't the first time, and it won't be the last: and she always gets out of it. Leave it in God's hands; there's nothing you can do about it, you poor girl. Even a man can't do anything about it, unless he's a soldier.

JOAN. But I can. My voices have said so.

FATHER (*laughing*). Oh, you can, can you? Dear me! You're sharper than all our great captains, of course, who can't do anything these days except be beaten every time they fight?

JOAN. Yes, father.

FATHER. Yes, father! Perhaps you're not a bad girl, but worse. You're a mad, idiot girl. What do you think you can do then, poor idiot?

JOAN. What my Voices tell me. I can ask the Squire of Beaudricourt for an armed escort. And when I've got my escort, I can go straight to the Dauphin at Chinon, to tell him that he's the rightful King; and I can lead him out at the head of the soldiers to save Orleans; and then I can persuade him to be consecrated with holy oil by the Archbishop, and then we can hurl the English into the sea.

FATHER (*suddenly understanding*). Now you're explaining yourself, at last, you filthy little slut! You want to go off with the soldiers, like the lowest of the low?

JOAN (*smiling mysteriously*). No, father, like the highest under God, riding first into the battle, and not looking back until I have saved France. (*Suddenly sad.*) And after that is done, what happens is God's will.

FATHER. I've heard enough shameless lying! I won't stand any more of it! I'll teach you what happens to girls who

14

go chasing after soldiers, pretending to save France!

He savagely and unmercifully beats and kicks her.

JOAN (*crying*). Stop, father, stop! stop!

The FATHER *has taken off his belt, and starts to leather her, gasping with effort.*

LADVENU (*rising, very pale*). This must be stopped! He means to injure her.

CAUCHON (*gently*). We can do nothing, Brother Ladvenu. At this part of the story we have never met Joan; we don't get to know her until the trial. We can only act our parts, each his own, good or bad, as they are written, and in his turn. And later on, you know, we shall do worse things than this to her. (*He turns to* WARWICK.) This domestic scene is not very pleasant to witness, my lord?

WARWICK (*with a gesture*). Why not? We're firm believers in corporal punishment in England; it forms the character. I myself have been flogged many times as a boy; and I took it extremely well.

The FATHER, *at last too exhausted to go on, wipes the sweat off his forehead, and shouts at* JOAN, *lying crumpled at his feet.*

FATHER. There! you carrion! Do you still want to save France? (*He turns to the others, rather ashamed of himself.*) Well, sirs, what would you have done in my place if your daughter had said that to you?

MOTHER (*coming forward*). Have you killed her?

FATHER. Not this time. But if she talks any more about going off with the soldiers, I'll drown that girl of yours in the river with my own hands, do you hear me? And if I'm nowhere about, I give her brother full permission to do it for me. (*He strides off.*)

The MOTHER *bends over* JOAN *and dries her face.*

15

MOTHER. Joan, my little Joan, my little Joan. Did he hurt you?

JOAN (*giving a pathetic smile when she recognises her* MOTHER). Yes. He meant me to feel it.

MOTHER. He's your father, Joan; you must bear it patiently.

JOAN (*in a small voice*). I do bear it, mother. I prayed while he beat me: prayed that our heavenly Father would forgive him.

MOTHER (*shocked*). Our heavenly Father doesn't have to forgive fathers for beating their daughters. It's their right.

JOAN. And I prayed for him to understand.

MOTHER (*fondling her*). Understand what, my silly one? Why did you have to tell him all this nonsense?

JOAN (*in agony*). Someone has to understand; otherwise I'm by myself, and I have to face them alone!

MOTHER (*rocking her in her arms*). Now, now, now, you don't have to upset yourself. You remember when you were little, we would rock away your nightmares together. But now you're nearly a woman: nearly too big to hold in my arms any more, and I can tell you it's no good breaking your heart to make men understand anything. All you can do is say " yes " to whatever they think, and wait till they've gone out to the fields. Then you can be mistress in your own house again. Your father's a good man; but if I didn't trick him sometimes for his own good I don't know where we should be. Who is it, Joan? You can tell your mother. Don't you even know his name, perhaps? And yet I don't know but it must be someone in the village. Why, your father might even agree to him; he's not against a good marriage for you. We might even be able to persuade him he chose the boy himself.

16

the poor old stupid. You know what men are: roar a
lot, and lay down the law, and bang you about; but, the
same as with a bull, you can lead them by the nose.

JOAN. It isn't marriage that I have to think of, mother.
The blessed St. Michael has told me I should leave the
village, put on a man's clothes, and go and find his
highness the Dauphin, to save the realm of France.

MOTHER (*severely*). Joan, I speak nicely and gently to you,
but I won't have you talking wickedness. And I won't
have you put on a man's clothes, not if you beg at my
grave. Have my daughter a man! You let me catch you,
my goodness!

JOAN. But, mother, I should have to, if I'm to ride horseback with the soldiers. It's the blessed St. Michael who
says so.

MOTHER. I don't care what the blessed St. Michael says,
you shall never go off on a horse. Joan of Arc on a
horse! It would be the talk of the village.

JOAN. But the lady of Vaucouleurs rides a horse to hawking.

MOTHER. You will not ride a horse, never! It isn't the
station of life you were born to. Such grand ideas,
indeed!

JOAN. But if I don't ride a horse, how can I lead the
soldiers?

MOTHER. And you won't go with the soldiers, either, you
wicked girl! I'd rather see you cold and dead. You
see, how you make me talk the same as your father.
There are some things we feel the same about. A
daughter spins, and scrubs, and stays at home. Your
grandmother never left this village, and neither have I,
and neither will you, and when you have a daughter of
your own, neither will she. (*She suddenly bursts into*

17

tears). Going off with the soldiers! Do you want to kill me?

JOAN (*throwing herself into her mother's arms, crying too*). No, mother!

MOTHER. You do: I can see you do. And you'll destroy yourself in the end if you don't soon get these thoughts out of your head. (*Exit.*)

> JOAN *straightens herself up, still in tears, while her* MOTHER *goes back to the* CROWD.

JOAN. You see, St. Michael, it isn't possible; they won't ever understand. No one will. It is better that I should give up at once. Our Lord has said that we have to obey our father and mother. (*She speaks with the voice of the Archangel.*)

——But, first, Joan, you have to obey God.

——But if God commands the impossible?

——Then you have to attempt the impossible, calmly and quietly. It is a cause for pride, Joan, that God gives you something of His burden to carry.

After a pause.

——My Lord, do you think our Saviour can want a daughter to make her parents weep, and leave them alone to break their hearts, perhaps to die? That's hard to understand.

——He has said, I come to bring not peace, but a sword. I am come to set the brother against the sister and the son against the father. God came to bring struggle, Joan; not to make the way easy, but to make the way harder. He doesn't ask the impossible of everybody, but He does ask it of you. That is all. (JOAN *looks up, and says simply.*)—Well, I will go.

A VOICE (*from somewhere out of the shadows behind*). Proud and arrogant!

JOAN (*disturbed*). Who is calling me proud and arrogant?

(*After a pause, in the voice of the Archangel.*)

——It was you, Joan. And when you begin to do what God is asking, it will be what the world calls you. But if you give yourself humbly into the hands of God, you can bear this blame of pride.

——It is heavy to bear, my Lord!

——Yes, it is heavy. But God knows that you are strong.

A silence. She looks straight in front of her, and suddenly becomes a little girl again, happy and decided.

All right, then. It's all decided. I shall go and find my Uncle Durand. With him I always get my own way. He's easy to manage as a tame sparrow. I shall kiss him on both cheeks, and on the top of his head, and sit on his lap, and he will say " Oh Lord, Oh Lord," and take me to Vaucouleurs!

BROTHER You're a silly donkey! Why did you have to go and tell the old people all that stuff? Next time, if you give me a ha'penny, I won't say a word about where I saw you.

JOAN (*leaping cheerfully at him*). Oh, so it was you who told them, you beastly little pig? Sneak, sneak, I'll give you a tweak! Tell tales out of school, duck him in a muddy pool! There's your halfpenny, lardy-head. Tell-tale-tit, your tongue shall be split, and all the children in the town shall have a little bit!

They fight like urchins. She chases straight across the stage towards BEAUDRICOURT *who has come forward to take the centre of the stage.*

19

BEAUDRICOURT. Well, what is it? What does she want? What is it you want, you infernal nuisance? What's this nonsensical story I hear——

> JOAN *collides head first with* BEAUDRICOURT'S *great paunch. He is half winded, gives a yell of pain, grabs her by the arm and lifts her level with his nose, apoplectic with rage.*

What the devil do you want, you horrible mosquito? What the devil do you mean, playing the fool outside my gates for three days on end? What the devil are these tales you've been telling the guards until their eyes pop out as far as their noses?

JOAN (*breathless with her running and poised on tip-toe in the arms of the giant*). I want a horse, my lord, a man's clothes, and an escort, to go to Chinon to see his highness the Dauphin.

BEAUDRICOURT. And my boot, you want that, too, of course?

JOAN. If you like, my lord, and a good clout, as long as I get the horse as well.

BEAUDRICOURT (*still holding her*). You know about me and you know what I want; the village girls have told you all about it, haven't they? They come along to see me, usually to beg for the life of a brother, or their old father who's been caught poaching on my lands. If the girl is pretty, I always hook him down off the gallows, being amiable at heart. If she's ugly, I hang the old chap, to make an example of him. But it's always the pretty ones who come; they manage to dig up one in the family somehow; with the admirable result that I have a fine reputation for benevolence in the neighbourhood. So now you know the rate of exchange, and we can come to terms.

20

JOAN (*simply*). I don't know what you're trying to say, my lord. The blessed St. Michael sent me to you.

BEAUDRICOURT (*crossing himself anxiously with his free hand*). You don't have to bring the saints into this. That was all right for the guards, to get you in to see me. But now you're here, and you can leave the saints in their proper places. And I wouldn't be surprised if you get your horse. An old jade for a young maid; it's a reasonable bargain. Are you a virgin?

JOAN. Yes, my lord.

BEAUDRICOURT (*looking at her all the time*). I agree to the horse.

JOAN. That isn't all I want, my lord.

BEAUDRICOURT. A greedy child, I see! Well, go on; you're amusing me. If I pay well for my pleasures it helps me to believe I really want them. You understand where this conversation is leading?

JOAN (*frankly*). No, my lord.

BEAUDRICOURT. Splendid. The bed's no place for brains. What else do you want beside the horse? The taxes are coming in very well this autumn; I don't mind being generous.

JOAN. An escort of men-at-arms, my lord, to accompany me to Chinon.

BEAUDRICOURT (*freeing her, changing his tone*). Now listen to me, if we're to get on together: I may be easygoing, but I won't stand any impudence. I'm the master here and you're using up my patience fast. I can just as well have you whipped for forcing your way in here, and send you home with nothing except the marks on your backside. So behave yourself. Why do you want to go to Chinon?

21

JOAN. To find his highness the Dauphin.

BEAUDRICOURT. Well, well, you mean to get on! Why not the Duke of Burgundy while you're about it? In theory, you might have a sporting chance with him: the Duke's as hot as a buck rabbit. Whereas, as you probably know, the Dauphin when it comes to war and women . . . I don't know what you expect to get from him.

JOAN. An army, my lord, which I can lead to Orleans.

BEAUDRICOURT. Ah: if you're mad it's another thing altogether. I'm not getting involved in any scandal. (*He turns to the crowd upstage.*) Hey, there, Boudousse!

   A GUARD *comes forward.*

Take her away and give her a ducking, and then lock her up. You can send her back to her father tomorrow evening. But no beating, I don't want any trouble; the girl's mad.

JOAN (*calmly, held by the* GUARD). You can lock me up, my lord: I don't mind that; but when they let me out tomorrow evening I shall come back again. So it would be simpler if you let me talk to you now.

BEAUDRICOURT. Ten million thunders! Don't I frighten you?

JOAN. No, my lord. Not at all.

BEAUDRICOURT (*to the* GUARD). Get back to your post! you don't need to stand about, listening to this.

   The GUARD *goes, and when he has gone* BEAUDRICOURT *asks uneasily.*

And why don't I frighten you? I frighten everybody.

JOAN (*quietly*). You are very good, my lord.

BEAUDRICOURT. Good? Good? I've told you, that depends on the price.

JOAN. And what's more, very intelligent. There are many people I will have to convince before I can do everything my Voices want; so its lucky the first person I have to deal with, the one everything really depends on, should turn out to be the most intelligent.

BEAUDRICOURT (*slightly puzzled, asks in a casual voice while he pours himself some wine*). You're an odd girl, in your way. How did you come to notice that I'm intelligent?

JOAN. Because you're very handsome, my lord.

BEAUDRICOURT (*with a furtive glance into the metal mirror beside him*). Oh, tush! I suppose, twenty years ago, I might say that I pleased the ladies; and I've taken care of myself, not let myself get too old too soon; that's all it is.—It's quite peculiar and unsettling to have a conversation like this with a farm girl I've never heard of, who happens to drop in like a stray kitten. (*He sighs.*) On the whole I vegetate here. My lieutenants are a poor bunch: hardly a brain between them. And while we're on the subject, what's this connection you find between intellect and beauty? I've usually heard quite the opposite: handsome people are always stupid; that's the general opinion.

JOAN. That's the opinion of the plain people, who like to believe God can't manage both things at once.

BEAUDRICOURT (*flattered*). Ah, well, you've made a point there. But then, take myself for example. I know, as you so kindly say, I'm not one of the plain people; but I wonder sometimes, am I, after all, very intelligent? No no, don't protest. It's a question I have to ask now and again. I can tell you this, between ourselves, as you're not anyone in particular. Obviously I'm more intelligent than my lieutenants, that's only natural, being officer in command. If that wasn't an established fact there wouldn't be an army at all. But even so, I sometimes meet with problems which I find very troublesome. They ask me to decide something, some tactical or administrative point, and quite suddenly, I don't know why, my mind is a blank. There it is, nothing but a sort of fog. Mark you, nobody knows that. I get out of it, without my face showing any change of expression; I make a decision all right. And that's the essential thing when you're in command, of course: make a decision, whatever it is. Until you've had some experience you're apt to get flustered: but you realise after a bit, it all amounts to the same thing, whatever you decide. Still, I should like to see myself doing better. Vaucouleurs, as you see, is of no great size. I'm looking forward to the day when I make a really important decision: one of those momentous decisions, of great consequence to the nation: not a question of somebody who hasn't paid his taxes, or half a dozen prisoners to be hanged: but something a bit exceptional, which would get me noticed and talked about higher up. (*He stops dreaming, and looks at her.*) I don't know what in the world I'm doing telling you all this. You can't do anything about it, and God help you, you're half crazy into the bargain.

JOAN (*smiling gently*). I know why. I knew it would happen, because they told me so. Listen, Robert——

BEAUDRICOURT (*startled*). What are you doing calling me by my Christian name?

JOAN. It's God's name for you, Robert. Now listen, Robert, and don't bluster again, because it isn't any use. What is the important decision, which will get you noticed and talked about higher up? I can tell you, Robert. It's me.

24

BEAUDRICOURT. What are you talking about?

JOAN (*coming to him*). I'll tell you, if you'll listen. First of all, you have to stop thinking of me as a girl, that's what is getting you confused. And I don't mean much to you anyway, do I?

He hesitates, afraid of being cheated; she flares up.

Robert, if you want to help yourself, you have to help me, too! When I tell you the truth, acknowledge it and say Yes: otherwise we shall never get anywhere.

BEAUDRICOURT (*muttering, rather shamefaced*). Well, no . . .

JOAN (*severely*). What do you mean, no?

BEAUDRICOURT. I mean, yes, it's true. I'm not particular about you. (*Adding politely.*) Though, mind you, you're a pretty enough little thing. . . .

JOAN. All right, you don't have to think you've upset me. I'm very happy the point is cleared up. And now you can imagine you have already given me the suit of clothes I asked for, and we can discuss things together, sensibly and calmly, as man to man.

BEAUDRICOURT (*still suspicious*). Discuss what?

JOAN (*sitting on the edge of the table, finishing the dregs in the wine glass*). Your own important decision, my splendid Robert. Your great achievement which will make everyone take notice of you. Think of all of them, there at Bourges. They don't know whether they're praying or cursing, or which saint to turn to next. The English are everywhere. And you know the French army. Good boys, who have still got fight in them, but they're discouraged. They've got it into their heads that the English will always be the strongest, and there's nothing to be done. Dunois the Bastard; he's a good captain; intelligent, which is rare in the army, but no one listens to him

25

any more, and he's getting tired of it. So he spends his days having a high old time with the women in the camp (and that's something else I shall have to deal with): and he's far too cock-a-hoop, like all bastards. "The affairs of France aren't his concern: let that milksop Charles get his country out of the tangle for himself." Then there's La Hire, and there's Xantrailles: prize angry bulls: they always want to charge in head first, slashing and thrusting like old heroes in the chronicles. They belong among the champions of single combat, who don't understand how to use their cannons, and always get killed to no purpose whatever, the way they did at Agincourt. They're wonderful at getting killed, but it isn't any help. That's true, isn't it, Robert. You can't treat war like a tournament. You have to win. You have to be cunning. (*She touches her forehead.*) You have to wage it here. With all your intelligence, Robert, you know that better than I do.

BEAUDRICOURT. I've always said so. Nowadays we don't think enough. Take my lieutenants: always spoiling for a fight, and that's all they can think of. And the men who know how to think get overlooked; nobody dreams of using them.

JOAN. Nobody. So they have to think for themselves. It's a lucky thing you have had such a tremendous idea. It's certain to alter everything.

BEAUDRICOURT (*uneasily*). I have an idea?

JOAN. Don't question it, Robert; be very proud of it. Your brain is working at great speed, clearly and concisely. It's a sad thing to think that, in the whole of France at this moment, no one sees things clearly, except you.

BEAUDRICOURT. You believe so?

JOAN. I tell you so.

BEADRICOURT. And what is it I see?

JOAN. You see simply that the people of France have to be given a spirit and a faith. And it so happens that you have with you at this moment a young country girl. St. Michael has appeared to her, and St. Catherine and St. Margaret, or at least she says they have. You are not so sure about it, but for the time being it's not important. And this is where you show yourself to be so remarkable. You say to yourself: Here's a little peasant girl, of no consequence at all; all right. If by any chance she really has been sent by God, then nothing could stop her, and it can't be proved one way or the other whether God sent her or not. She certainly got in to see me, without my permission, and I've been listening to her for half an hour; nobody could deny that. And then, like a sword of lightning, the idea strikes home to you. You say to yourself: If she has the power to convince me, why shouldn't she convince the Dauphin and Dunois and the Archbishop? They're men, just as I'm a man; as a matter of fact, between ourselves, rather less intelligent. Moreover, why shouldn't she convince our soldiers that the English in the main are exactly like themselves, half courage and half a wish to save their skins; pummel them hard enough at the right moment, and you send them staggering out of Orleans. It's magnificent how you marshal the whole situation in your mind. What our fellows need, you are saying to yourself: what they need is someone to rouse their spirit and prove to them that God is still with them. This is where you show yourself a born leader, Robert.

BEAUDRICOURT (*pitifully*). You think that?

JOAN. I know it. And very soon so will everyone else. Like all great politicians, you're a realist, Robert. You say to
27

yourself: I, Beaudricourt, have my doubts about her coming from God, but I'll send her off to them, and if they think she is, it will have the same effect whether it's true or false. By a stroke of good luck my courier is leaving for Bourges tomorrow morning——

BEAUDRICOURT. Who told you that? It's a secret.

JOAN. I found it out. (*She continues.*) I pick half a dozen strong men for an escort, give her a horse and send her off with the courier. At Chinon, as far as I can see, she will work things out for herself. (*She looks at him admiringly.*) My word, my word, Robert!

BEAUDRICOURT. What?

JOAN. You have a marvellous intelligence to think of all that.

BEAUDRICOURT (*wiping his forehead, worn out*). Yes.

JOAN. Only, please give me a quiet horse, because I don't know how to ride one yet.

BEAUDRICOURT (*delighted*). You're going to break your neck, my girl!

JOAN. I don't think so. St. Michael will hold me on. I tell you what, Robert: I'll have a wager with you. I'll bet you a suit of clothes—the man's clothes which you still haven't said you'll give me—against a punch on the nose. Bring two horses into the courtyard and we'll gallop them together. If I fall off, you can lose faith in me. Is that fair? (*She offers him her hand.*) Agreed? And whoever doesn't pay up is a man of mud!

BEAUDRICOURT (*getting up*). Agreed! I need to move about a bit. I wouldn't have believed how tiring it is to think so much. (*He calls.*) Boudousse!
Enter the GUARD.

GUARD. Do I take her away and give her a ducking, sir?

BEAUDRICOURT. No, you idiot! You fetch her some breeches, and bring us a couple of horses. We're taking a gallop together.

GUARD. What about the Council, sir? It's four o'clock.

BEAUDRICOURT. It can wait till tomorrow. Today I've used my brains quite enough.

He goes. JOAN *passes the astonished* GUARD *and sticks out her tongue. They lose themselves in the crowd up stage.*

WARWICK (*to* CAUCHON). I can see this girl had quality. Very entertaining, to watch her playing the old fish, didn't you think so?

CAUCHON. Rather too crude for my taste, my lord. Something subtler than that will be needed when she comes to deal with Charles.

WARWICK. My lord Bishop, the tricks that you and I use in our way of business aren't so remarkably different from hers. Whether we're ruling the world with a mace or a crozier, in the long run, we do it by persuading fools that what we make them think is their own opinion. No need for any intervention of God in that. Which is why I found it so entertaining. (*He bows politely towards the* BISHOP.) Entertaining, at least, if one isn't professionally concerned, of course, as you are. Have you faith yourself, my lord Bishop? Forgive my bluntness; but between ourselves. I'm interested to know.

CAUCHON (*simply*). A child's faith, my lord. And that is why I shall make problems for you during the trial, and why we shall go as far as ever we can to save Joan, even though we have been sincere collaborators with the English rule, which seemed to us then the only reasonable solution to chaos. It was very easy for those who were

29

at Bourges to call us traitors, when they had the protection of the French army. We were in occupied Rouen.

WARWICK. I don't like the word "occupied": You forget the Treaty of Troyes. You were quite simply on His Majesty's territory.

CAUCHON. In the midst of His Majesty's army, and the execution of His Majesty's hostages; submitting to the curfew, and the condescension of His Majesty's food-supplies. We were men, with the frailty of men, who wanted to go on living, and yet at the same time to save Joan if we could. It was not in any way a happy part that we were called upon to fill.

WARWICK (*smiling*). There was nothing to stop you becoming martyrs, my dear fellow, if that would have made it more inspiring for you. My eight hundred soldiers were quite ready.

CAUCHON. We knew it. They took great pleasure in shouting their insults at us, hammering on the door with the butts of their halberds, to remind us they were there. We temporised for nine months before we would deliver Joan up to you; this little girl, forsaken by everyone; nine months to make her say Yes. Future times will be pleased to say we were barbarous. But I fancy, for all their fine principles, they will take to expediency faster than we did; in every camp.

WARWICK. Nine months, that's quite true. What a difficult confinement this trial has been. Our Holy Mother Church takes her time, when she's asked to give birth to a small matter of policy. But the nightmare is over. The mother and child are both doing well.

CAUCHON. I have pondered deeply over these things, my lord. The health of the mother, as you put it, is our one

30

concern. And that is why, when we saw there could be no alternative, we sacrificed the child in good faith. Ever since that day of Joan's arrest, God has been dead to us. Neither she, whatever she may imagine, nor we, certainly, have heard Him any more. We have gone on, following our daily custom; our pre-eminent duty, to defend the old house, this great and wise human building which is all that remains to us in the absence of God. From the time we were fifteen years old, we were taught how to defend it. Joan had no such help, and yet, though her faith fell on dreadful days, when she was left alone by men and by God, she also has gone on, recovering at once after the single moment when she weakened, bearing herself with her curious mixture of humility and insolence, of grandeur and good sense, even up to execution and death. We weren't able to understand it then; we had our eyes buried in our mother's skirts, like children grown old. And yet, precisely in this loneliness, in the desert of a vanished God, in the privation and misery of the animal, the man is indeed great who continues to lift his head. Greatly alone.

WARWICK. Yes, well, no doubt. But if our business is politics we can't afford to brood about such men. We seem fated, as a rule, to meet them among the people we condemn to execution.

CAUCHON (*quietly, after a pause*). It is a consolation to me sometimes to think of those old priests who, though they were deeply offended by her insolent answers, nevertheless, even with English swords at their back, tried for nine months not to commit the irreparable.

WARWICK. Enough of fine phrases, Bishop. Nothing is irreparable in politics. I tell you we shall raise a handsome statue to her in London one day, when the right time comes.

31

He turns towards the people of Chinon, who have been putting up a small palace set during this conversation.

But now let's come to Chinon, my lord. I've got a profound disrespect for that lounging little idler, Charles, but he's a character who never fails to amuse me.

CHARLES *is with the two Queens and* AGNES SOREL.

AGNES. But Charles, it's impossible! You can't let me appear at the ball looking such a frump. Your mistress in one of last year's steeple-hats.

QUEEN. And your Queen, Charles! The Queen of France! What would they say?

CHARLES (*playing cup-and-ball, dropping into his throne*). They would say the King of France isn't worth a farthing. Which is quite right.

QUEEN. And think how the English court would laugh! The Duchess of Bedford, and Gloucester's wife, to say nothing of the Cardinal of Winchester's mistress! Now there's someone who knows how to dress.

AGNES. Imagine, Charles, if they're wearing our newest fashions over there before we are!

CHARLES. At least they pay for them. Fashion is practically the only thing we can sell them: our fashions and our cooking. They are the only things which still give us some prestige with the foreigners.

YOLANDE. We have to defend this prestige. The girls aren't altogether wrong, Charles. It's most important there should be no question at this ball that ladies of the court of France are the best dressed women in the world. No one has ever been able to decide, remember, exactly where triviality begins. A steeple-hat the English have never seen before might be as good as a great victory.

CHARLES (*with a dry laugh*). A victory which isn't going to stop them making off with Orleans, mother-in-law! According to the latest reports, Orleans is lost. And you think we should counter-attack with a new fashion.

AGNES. Certainly. You've no idea what a dangerous blow it will be to their confidence. If you want a victory, Charles, here is one you can have for nothing.

CHARLES. For nothing? You make me laugh! How much did you say these steeple-hats would come to?

AGNES. Six thousand francs, my darling. That's next to nothing, when you remember they're completely embroidered with pearls. And the pearls are a good investment. When the steeple-hat isn't fashionable any more you can always sell the pearls at a profit and put it towards the army's back pay.

CHARLES. Six thousand francs! But where do you think I can find six thousand francs, you poor little fool?

QUEEN (*softly*). Twelve thousand francs, Charles, because there are two of us, remember. You wouldn't want your mistress to be better dressed than your wife.

CHARLES (*raising his hands to heaven*). Twelve thousand francs! They've gone out of their minds!

AGNES. Of course there's a simpler model, but I wouldn't advise it. You would forfeit the moral effect we should have on the stupid English. And that, after all, is the effect we're after.

CHARLES. Twelve thousand francs! Enough to pay three-quarters of Dunois's army. I don't understand how you can encourage them, mother-in-law, a woman of your good judgment.

YOLANDE. It's because I'm a woman of good judgment that I support them, Charles. Have you ever found me opposing anything that might be for your good or the dignity of the throne? I am the mother of your Queen, and yet it was I who introduced you to Agnes when I saw clearly how it might help you.

QUEEN. Please, mother, don't brag about it!

YOLANDE. Daughter, Agnes is a very charming girl who perfectly knows her place. It was quite as important to you as to me, that Charles should decide to become a man. And the kingdom had even more need of it than we had. A little more pride, dear girl; at the moment you have thoughts like a tradesman's wife! Before Charles could become a man he had to be given a woman.

QUEEN (*acidly*). I was a woman, it seems to me, and his wife, what is more.

YOLANDE. I don't want to wound you, my dearest girl: but only slightly a woman. I can say this to you, because I was very much the same. Good sense, intelligence—more than you have—but that was all. Which is why I was always willing that the King, your father, should have his mistresses. Be his Queen, run his house, give him a son and heir and leave the rest to other people. We can't do everything. And anyway, love is scarcely an honest woman's concern. We don't do well at it. Besides, you will thank me later on: one sleeps so much better alone. And Charles is far more manly since he knew Agnes. You are more manly, aren't you, Charles?

CHARLES. Yesterday I said " No " to the Archbishop. He tried to scare me, he sent La Tremouille in first to roar at me, and then he threatened to excommunicate me. All the old tricks. But I held firm.

AGNES. And thanks to whom?

CHARLES. Thanks to Agnes! We had rehearsed the whole scene in bed.

YOLANDE. What did the Archbishop want? You didn't tell me.

CHARLES (*caressing* AGNES *absent-mindedly*). I can't remember. To give up Paris to the Duke of Burgundy, or something of the sort, in return for a year's truce. I might say it wouldn't really have meant anything at all. The Duke's in Paris already. But it was a matter of principle: Paris is France, and France is mine. At least I encourage myself to believe it is. So I said " No ". The Archbishop made such a great fuss about it, the Duke must have promised him a pretty good sum.

AGNES. And what would have happened, Charles dear, if you had said " yes " in spite of me?

CHARLES. You would have had a headache for a week, and although, I suppose, if I had to, I could do without Paris, I couldn't do without you.

AGNES. Well, then, my darling, if I have helped you to save Paris, you can surely buy me the new steeple-hat, and one for your little Queen, too, because you have said some very hurtful things to her, without noticing it, as usual, you bad boy. You don't want me to be ill for a whole week, do you? You wouldn't know what to do with yourself.

CHARLES. All right, then, order your steeple-hats. I always have to say "yes" to somebody, if it isn't the Archbishop, it's you. But I may as well tell you, I haven't the least idea how I'm going to pay for them.

AGNES. You're going to sign a draft on the Treasury Charles, and we will see what happens later. Come along, little Majesty, we will try them on together. Would you rather have this rose-coloured one, or the sky-blue? I think myself the rose is the one which will suit you best.

CHARLES. What do you mean? Have you got them already?

AGNES. You're very slow at understanding, my dearest! Surely you can see, if we were to have them in time for the ball we had to order them a month ago? But we were so sure you would say " yes ", weren't we, Your Majesty? You shall see what a sensation this causes in London! It's a great victory for France, you know, Charles!

They take to their heels.

CHARLES (*sitting back on his throne again*). There's nothing you can do but laugh, the way they harp on victories. La Tremouille, Dunois, they're all the same! There is always going to be a great victory. But everything has to be paid for, including great victories, these days. And suppose I can't afford a great victory? Suppose France is above my means? (*He takes his writing desk, muttering.*) Ah well, we shall see! I can always sign a draft on the Treasury. Let's hope it will please the tradesmen. The Treasury is empty, but there's nothing on this paper to say so. (*He turns towards the* QUEEN YOLANDE.) You wouldn't like a steeple-hat too, while I'm doing it? You needn't mind saying so. My signature isn't worth the ink it's written in.

YOLANDE (*coming to him*). I'm past the age for steeple-hats, Charles. I want something else.

CHARLES (*wearily*). To make me a great King, I know! It gets very boring in the end, everybody wants to make me a great King. Even Agnes. Even in bed. Imagine how jolly that is. I wish you would all try and get it into your heads, I'm an unimportant, insignificant Valois, and to make a King of me would need a miracle. I know my grandfather Charles was a great king; but he lived before the war when everything was much cheaper. Besides, he was rich. But my father and mother spent it all, so

36

whether you like it or not, I can't afford to be a great king; I haven't got the money, and I haven't got the courage; you all know I haven't. Courage is far too dangerous in a world full of bullying brutes. That fat pig La Tremouille was in a raging temper the other day, and drew his sword on me. We were alone together: nobody there to defend me. He was quite prepared to give me a jab with it, the beastly hooligan! I only just had time to dodge behind the throne. So you see what we've come to. Drawing his sword on the King! I should have sent for the constable to arrest him, except that unfortunately he is the constable, and I'm not sure that I am the King. That's why they treat me like this; they know that I may be only a bastard.

YOLANDE. It's nobody but yourself, Charles, who is always saying so.

CHARLES. When I look at the legitimate faces all round me I hope I am a bastard. It's a charming day and age to live in, when a man isn't considered anybody unless he can brandish an eight-pound sword, and stroll about in a suit of armour which would sink a galleon. When they put it on me, I'm welded into the ground; a great help to my dignity. And I don't like fighting. I don't like hitting, and I don't like being hit. And what's more, if you want to know, I'm frightened of it. (*He turns towards her crossly.*) What other impossibilities do you want me to do?

YOLANDE. I want you to receive this girl from Vaucouleurs. She says God sent her; and furthermore she says she has come to deliver Orleans. The people can think and talk of nothing else, and they're only waiting now to hear that you agree to receive her.

CHARLES. Then they're going to find I'm not as ridiculous

as they think I am. Give audience to an eccentric peasant girl? Really, mother-in-law, for a woman of good sense you disappoint me.

YOLANDE. I've given you Agnes, because I thought it was for your good, Charles, though against my interest as a mother. Now I tell you to accept this girl from Domremy. She seems to possess some exceptional power, or so everybody says, which is a point to be considered.

CHARLES (*bored*). I don't like virgins. I know, you're going to tell me again that I'm not virile enough. But they frighten me. And, anyway, I have Agnes, who still pleases me quite well enough. Don't think I'm reproaching you, but for someone who is a queen and my mother-in-law, you have a very remarkable vocation.

YOLANDE (*smiles*). You don't understand me, Charles, or else you're pretending not to. I'm asking you to take this peasant girl into your counsel, not into your bed.

CHARLES. In that case, in spite of all the respect I owe you, I have to tell you you're absolutely mad. Into my council, with the Archbishop, and La Tremouille, who believes that he sprang from Jupiter's thigh? Do you want them to knock my head off?

YOLANDE (*gently*). I think a peasant in your counsels is exactly what you all need. The nobility governs the kingdom, which is as it should be; God has entrusted it into their hands. But, without presuming to criticise the wisdom of providence, I wonder sometimes that he hasn't given them what he gives so generously to humbler men, a better measure of simplicity and common sense.

CHARLES (*ironically*). And courage!

YOLANDE (*gently*). And courage, Charles.

CHARLES. As far as I can understand you, you recommend turning the government over to the people? To the good people who have all the virtues. You've read the history of tyrants, I suppose?

YOLANDE. No, Charles. In my day, knowledge was not encouraged in young women.

CHARLES. But I've read it: the endless procession of horrors and scandals; and I amuse myself sometimes by imagining how the procession will go on in the future. They will certainly try what you recommend. They'll try everything. Men of the people will become masters of the kingdoms, maybe for centuries, the time it takes for a meteor to cross the sky; and that will be the time for massacres and the most monstrous errors. And what will they find, at the great account, when all is done? They'll find that not even the most vile, capricious, and cruel of the princes have cost the world as much as one of these virtuous men. Give France a powerful man of action, born of the people, whose ambition is to make the people happy, whatever it may entail, and see how they'll come to wish to God they had their poor lazy Charles back again, with his everlasting game of cup-and-ball. At least I've no theories about organizing the happy life. A negative virtue, perhaps, but more valuable than they realise yet.

YOLANDE. You should give up this cup-and-ball game, Charles, and this habit of sitting upside down on your throne. It's no behaviour for a king.

CHARLES. You would be sensible to let me be as I am. When the ball misses the cup, it drops on to my nose and nobody else's. But sit me on the throne the right way up, with the orb in one hand and the sceptre in the other, then whenever I make a mistake the ball will drop on everybody's nose.

39

Enter the ARCHBISHOP *and* LA TREMOUILLE. *He sits like a king on his throne.*

CHARLES. Archbishop, Constable, you've come at the perfect moment. I am starting to govern. You see I have here the orb and the sceptre.

ARCHBISHOP (*taking his eye-glass*). It's a cup-and-ball!

CHARLES. Unimportant. Archbishop; symbolism, after all. That isn't something I have to teach a prince of the Church. Your announced visit to me, my lord, must mean you wish for an audience.

ARCHBISHOP. I haven't come to be playful, Sire I know very well the minority opinion, which cares to intrigue and agitate on every possible occasion, is trying to persuade you to see this notorious peasant girl you have heard of. The Constable and I are here, Sire, to say it is not our intention to admit her.

CHARLES (*to* QUEEN YOLANDE). What did I tell you?—— I have taken note of what you recommend, my lord, and I shall consider what course to follow. Now you may go; the audience is over.

ARCHBISHOP. I will remind you, Sire, we are not here for your amusement.

CHARLES. Whenever I talk like a king for a moment, they always think I'm amusing myself. (*He lies back on his throne with the cup and ball.*) Very well, then; leave me to amuse myself in peace.

ARCHBISHOP. This girl's miraculous reputation is spreading across the country ahead of her; it was here before she arrived; it's already causing excitement in beseiged Orleans. God has taken her by the hand and leads her: this is the story. God has decided that she shall save France and drive the English back across the sea; and other such nonsense. God will expect you to receive her into the royal presence, and nothing is going to prevent her. I don't know why they're so anxious that God should concern Himself in their affairs. And naturally she has performed miracles; it would have surprised me more if she hadn't. A soldier called her I don't know what when she arrived at Chinon. She told him that he was wrong to swear, because soon he would be standing before his Redeemer. And an hour later this boorish fellow missed his footing, and fell into the well in the servants' yard, and drowned himself. That blundering step of a drunkard has done more for the girl's reputation than a great victory ever did for Dunois. Apparently the opinion is unanimous, from the lowest kennel-boy to the highest lady in your court: only this wretched girl can save us. A preposterous infatuation!——I speak to you, sir, of the gravest matters of the realm, and you play at cup-and-ball.

CHARLES. My lord, let us be clear about this. Do you want me to play at cup-and-ball, or do you want me to govern? (*He sits up.*) Do you want me to govern?

ARCHBISHOP (*disturbed*). Sir, we don't ask you to go as far as that. We wish you to notice and appreciate the efforts we are making . . .

CHARLES. I assure you, I notice them; I appreciate them; and I find them quite useless, my lord. Everyone expects me to see this girl, isn't it so?

ARCHBISHOP. I haven't said that!

CHARLES. Well, I'm not at all curious to see her. I'm not fond of new faces; we have to know too many people as it is. And messengers from God aren't usually very enlivening. But I want to be a good king, and content my

41

people. I shall see this peasant girl, if only to take the wind out of her sails. Have you spoken to her yourself, Archbishop?

ARCHBISHOP. I have other things to do, sir, when you consider that I carry the whole burden of the Kingdom's affairs.

CHARLES. Quite so. And I have nothing else to do except play at cup-and-ball. So I shall see her to save you the trouble: and I shall tell you frankly what I think of her. You can trust me to do that, my lord. I know you don't easily credit me with any qualities worth having, but at least you will agree that I'm a frivolous man: a quite useful condition for this interview. I'm very soon bored by anyone who takes himself seriously. I am going to receive this girl, and if she can make me want to listen to her talking about the welfare of the kingdom, which no one has ever done yet without making me yawn, then there's no doubt about her performing miracles.

ARCHBISHOP (*muttering*). A peasant girl in the presence of the king!

CHARLES (*simply*). You will remember, I think, that some of all kinds have been admitted to my presence. I don't mean M. de la Tremouille, who springs, of course, direct from Jupiter's thigh. But, for instance, yourself, my lord: —I think I remember being told you were the grandson of a wine merchant. There is no reproach in that. What could be more natural? You have carried the wine from your cellars to the altar. And as for myself, as you frequently have told me, it's a moot point whether I'm the son of a king. So we'd better not play the ancestry game, my lord, or we shall be making ourselves altogether ridiculous. (*To* QUEEN YOLANDE.) Come with me, and help me get ready for her. I've thought of a very amusing joke. We can disguise one of the pages in a royal doublet, if we can find one that isn't too shabby; sit him on the throne, which I am sure he will manage better than I can, and I shall hide myself in the crowd. Then we can listen to a solemn harangue from the messenger of God to a page-boy! It ought to be irresistible, don't you think so?

They go out.

ARCHBISHOP (*to* LA TREMOUILLE). Do we let him do it? It's a game to him, like everything else. It shouldn't be dangerous. And once he has seen her, the people may very well calm down again. In a fortnight they will have found some other messenger of God to infatuate them, and the girl will be forgotten.

LA TREMOUILLE. I command the army, Archbishop, and I can only tell you, the official doctor of the nation has nothing more to say. We're now entirely in the hands of the bone-setters, the faith-healers, the quacks. In other words, what you call messengers from God. What do we risk?

ARCHBISHOP (*anxiously*). Constable, wherever God concerns himself everything is a risk. If the unlikely should be true, and He really has sent this girl to us: if, in fact, He means to take our part, then our troubles are only beginning. We shall be shaken out of all custom and orthodoxy, contrive to win four or five battles, and then will come the problems, the complications. Long experience as a man, both in the church and in government, teaches me that never, never must we draw God's attention to us. It is better to remain very small, Constable, very small and unnoticed.

The COURTIERS *take their places with the* QUEENS; *a* PAGE *sits on the throne;* CHARLES *slips into the*

43

crowd. The ARCHBISHOP *concludes in an undertone.*
Everybody is grouped round the throne where the little
PAGE *sits;* CHARLES *is in the crowd.* JOAN *enters*
alone, looking very small and simple among the
armour and the court fashions. They make a way
for her to pass to the throne. She is about to kneel,
hesitates, blushes, looking at the PAGE.

YOLANDE (*whispering in her ear*). You must kneel, child,
before the king.

> JOAN *turns towards her, puzzled; then suddenly she*
> *looks at all the silent people who are watching her,*
> *and advances silently in the crowd, who make way*
> *for her. She goes towards* CHARLES, *who tries to*
> *hide from her. When he sees that she is about to*
> *reach him, he almost runs to hide behind the others,*
> *but she follows him, almost running, too. She finds*
> *him in a corner and falls on her knees.*

CHARLES (*embarrassed in the silence*). What do you want
with me?

JOAN. Gentle Dauphin, I am called Joan the Maid. God
has brought me to you, to tell you that you will be
anointed and crowned in the city of Rheims. You will
be viceroy of the King of Heaven, who is King of France.

CHARLES (*awkwardly*). Well, that is very nice. But Rheims
belongs to the English, I understand. How would I get
there?

JOAN (*still on her knees*). By your own strength, gentle
Dauphin; by beating them. We will start with Orleans,
and then we can go to Rheims.

LA TREMOUILLE (*coming up*). Little lunatic! Isn't that
what all the army commanders have been trying to do
for months? I am the head of them; I know something
about it. And they haven't got there.

44

JOAN (*getting up*). I will get there.

LA TREMOUILLE. Will you indeed? And how will you get there?

JOAN. With the help of God Who sends me.

LA TREMOUILLE. I see. So God has arranged for us to re-take Orleans?

JOAN. Yes, my lord; and to hunt the English out of France.

LA TREMOUILLE (*jeering*). A very beautiful thought! But God can't convey His own messages Himself? He has to have you to do it for Him?

JOAN. Yes, my lord.

ARCHBISHOP (*approaching her*). Young woman . . .

> JOAN *sees him, kneels and kisses the hem of his robe. He gives her his ring to kiss, and motions her to rise.*

You say that God wishes to deliver the kingdom of France. If such is indeed His will, He has no need of armies, or you to lead them.

JOAN. Oh, my lord, does God care for those who have no care? First the soldiers must fight, and then He will give the victory.

CHARLES. How did you recognise me without my crown?

JOAN. Gentle Dauphin, it was a good joke to put your crown on this boy, it doesn't take much to see that he's really a little nobody.

CHARLES. You're mistaken. The boy is the son of a great lord.

JOAN. Great lords are not the king.

CHARLES (*troubled*). Who told you I was the king? I don't look like a king.

JOAN. God told me, gentle Dauphin: Who appointed you from the beginning of time, through your father and your grandfather and all the line of kings, to be viceroy of His kingdom.

The ARCHBISHOP *and* LA TREMOUILLE *exchange a look of annoyance.*

ARCHBISHOP. Sire. The girl's answers are interesting: they show a remarkable good sense. But in a matter as delicate as this you cannot surround yourself with precautions too strict or thorough. A commission of learned theologians must question and examine her very closely. We will then discuss their report in Council, and decide if it is timely for you to give this girl a longer hearing. There's no need for her to importune you any further today. First of all I shall interrogate her myself. Come here, my daughter.

CHARLES. Not at all. (*He stops* JOAN.) Stay where you are. (*He turns to the* ARCHBISHOP, *taking* JOAN'S *hand to give himself courage.*) I was the one she recognised. I was the one she spoke to. I wish you to leave me alone with her: all of you.

ARCHBISHOP. This blunt dismissal, sir: it is quite extraordinary, it is improper! Apart from all else, you should at least think of your own security . . .

CHARLES (*fearful for a moment, but he looks at* JOAN *and pulls himself together*). I am the only judge of that. (*He recites:*) Through my father, my grandfather, and all the line of kings . . . (*He winks at* JOAN.) Isn't that right? (*He turns to the others, imperturbable.*) Leave us, my lords, when the king commands it.

They ALL *bow, and go.*

CHARLES *keeps his regal pose for a moment, and then explodes with laughter.*

They've gone, they've gone! Did I do that, or did you? It's the first time in my life I have ever made myself obeyed. (*He looks at her, suddenly anxious.*) I hope there is nothing in what the Archbishop was trying to suggest. You haven't come here to kill me? There isn't a knife hidden about you somewhere?

He looks at her, and she smiles gravely.

No. You reassure me. I had forgotten, among all these pirates in my court, how reassuring a smile could be. Are there many of you in my kingdom with such honest faces?

JOAN (*still smiling gravely*). Yes, sir, very many.

CHARLES. But I never see you. Only ruffians, hypocrites, and whores: my entourage. Though of course there's my little queen, who has a certain amount of charm but not many brains. (*He goes back to his throne, his feet on the rail, and sighs*). Well, there you are. I suppose now you have to start boring me. You're going to tell me to become a great king.

JOAN (*gently*). Yes, Charles.

CHARLES. Don't let's bother. We shall have to stay shut up here together for an hour at least, to impress them. If you talk to me about God and the kingdom of France for an hour, I shall never last out. I propose instead we talk about something quite different. Do you play cards?

JOAN (*opening her eyes wide*). I don't know what it is.

CHARLES. It's an amusing game they invented for Papa, to distract him during his illness. You'll see, I shall teach you. I've played so often now I've got tired of it, but I think you may like it if you've never played before. (*He goes to rummage about in a chest.*) I hope they haven't stolen them from me. They steal everything

47

here. And a pack of cards, you know, costs a lot of money. Only the royal princes have them. Mine were left to me by my father. I shall never have enough money to buy myself another pack. If those devils have stolen them . . . No, here they are. (*He returns with the cards.*) You knew Papa was mad, did you? Sometimes I hope I'm really his son, so that I can be sure I'm the true king; and then, at other times I hope I'm a bastard, so that I don't have to dread going mad before I'm thirty.

JOAN (*gently*). And which of the two would you prefer, Charles?

CHARLES (*turning in surprise*). Good heavens, are you calling me Charles? This is turning out to be a most surprising day. I believe I'm not going to be bored, for once; it's marvellous.

JOAN. Not now, Charles, or ever again.

CHARLES. Extraordinary.—Which of the two would I prefer? Well, I suppose on the days when I have some courage I would rather take the risk of going mad, and be the true king; and on the days when I haven't I would rather let everything go, and retire on my twopence-ha'penny to somewhere abroad, and live in peace. Have you met Agnes?

JOAN. No.

CHARLES (*shuffling the cards*). No, of course you haven't. Retiring wouldn't do for her. And I couldn't afford her then. She is always wanting me to buy her things.

JOAN (*suddenly grave*). And today: are you feeling brave today, Charles?

CHARLES. Today? (*He ponders a moment.*) Yes, it seems to me I feel fairly brave. Not very, but fairly. Well, you saw how I packed off the Archbishop.

JOAN. How would you like to be brave all the time, from today onwards?

CHARLES (*leaning forward, interested*). Do you mean you know the secret?

JOAN. Yes.

CHARLES. Are you some sort of a witch? You needn't be afraid to tell me; it isn't something I object to. I promise you I won't repeat it. Those executions horrify me. I was taken once to see them burn a heretic. I was sick all night.

JOAN (*smiling*). No, I'm not a witch, Charles. But I know the secret.

CHARLES. Would you sell it to me, without letting the others know about it? I'm not very well off, but I could make you a draft on the Treasury.

JOAN. I will give it to you, Charles.

CHARLES (*suspiciously*). For nothing?

JOAN. Yes.

CHARLES. Then I'm not interested. A secret is either no good, or far beyond my means. Disinterested people are too rare, at any price. (*He shuffles the cards.*) I've taken to behaving like a fool, so that I shall be left in peace, but I know more than you think I know. I'm not so easily gulled.

JOAN. You know too much.

CHARLES. Too much? You can never know too much.

JOAN. Sometimes; it is possible.

CHARLES. I have to defend myself. You would soon see, if you were here in my position! If you were alone, among a lot of brutes whose one idea is to stab you

49

when you are least expecting it, and if you've been born a weak sort of fellow, as I was, you would soon realise the only way to steer safely through it is by being more clever than they are. And I am; much more clever. Which is why I more or less hang on to my throne.

JOAN (*puts her hand on his arm*). I shall be with you now, defending you.

CHARLES. Do you think you will?

JOAN. And I'm strong. I'm not afraid of anything.

CHARLES (*sighing*). You're very lucky! (*He deals the cards.*) Sit down on the cushion; I'm going to teach you to play cards.

JOAN (*smiling, sitting close to the throne*). All right. And then I'll teach you something.

CHARLES. What?

JOAN. Not to be afraid. And not to know too much.

CHARLES. Now pay attention. You see the cards, and these pictures on them? There's something of everything here: knaves, queens, kings: the same as in the world: and here are the commoners: spades, hearts, clubs, diamonds. Those are the troops. There are plenty of them, you can lose as many as you like. You deal the cards without looking at them, and fate either gives you a good hand, or a bad hand, and then the battle begins. The higher cards can capture the lower cards. Which do you think is the strongest?

JOAN. The king is.

CHARLES. Well, he is almost the strongest, but there's one stronger still. This card here, for instance, the single heart. Do you know what it's called?

JOAN. God, of course: because He's the only one who commands kings.

CHARLES (*annoyed*). No, it isn't at all. For goodness sake let God alone for five minutes. For the time being we're playing cards. It's called the ace.

JOAN. Then the game of cards is ridiculous. What can be stronger than a king, except God?

CHARLES. The ace, in fact. The ace, or God if you like; but there's one in each camp. You see: ace of hearts, ace of spades, ace of clubs, ace of diamonds. One for each of them. You're not so intelligent as I thought you were. Do you think the English don't say their prayers, as well as us? And, what's more, to a God who protects them, and gives them victories over us. And my cousin, the Duke of Burgundy, he has a God for Burgundy, in just the same way: a smallish one, maybe, but a bold one, a cunning one, who gets my cousin out of difficulties very well. God is with everybody, my girl. He marks the points, and keeps the score. But, in the long run, He plumps for the people who have the most money and the biggest armies. So why do you imagine He should be with France, now that France has got nothing at all?

JOAN. Perhaps for that reason: because she has nothing at all, Charles.

CHARLES (*shrugging his shoulders*). You don't know Him!

JOAN. I do. God isn't with the strongest; He is with the bravest. There's the difference. God hasn't any love for cowards.

CHARLES. Then He doesn't love me. And if He doesn't love me, why do you expect me to love Him? All He had to do was to give me some courage. I don't ask for anything better.

JOAN (*severely*). Do you think He's your nurse, with no one else to think about but you? Why can't you make the best of what you have got; I know He has made you weak in the legs. . . .

CHARLES. You've noticed that? He ought to have managed better than that. Particularly with the present fashions. It's because of my legs that Agnes can't bring herself to love me. If He had only an eye for proportion, and hadn't given me my big knees as well. . . .

JOAN. Well, I grant you that. He didn't go to much trouble over your knees. But there was something else that more concerned Him; His eye was on your head and your heart, Charles, where you most resemble Him. And there it is He makes you free, to be whatever you will. You can use them to play cards, or to outmanœuvre the Archbishop for a time, though in the end you have to pay for it; or else you can use them to make the house of Valois glorious again, and remake the kingdom. Your little queen gave you a son, Charles. What are you going to leave the boy when you die? This wretched scrap of France, nibbled by the English? If so, when he grows up, the boy will be able to say, as you did just now, that God hasn't any interest in him. You are God, Charles, to your little son; and you have to take care of him.

CHARLES (*groans*). But I keep telling you, everything frightens me.

JOAN (*coming nearer to him*). You shall have the secret now, Charles. But don't give me away when I tell you first that everything frightens me, too. Do you know why M. de la Tremouille isn't afraid of anything?

CHARLES. Because he is strong.

52

JOAN. No. Because he is stupid. He never imagines anything. Wild boars, and bulls, and barrel-headed oxen
are never afraid of anything, either. And I tell you this:
it has been even more complicated for me to get to
you than it will be for you to get to Orleans and refashion
your kingdom. I had to explain to my father, and that
was a bad enough beginning. He wouldn't believe I
wanted anything, except to go dragging off after the
soldiers; and so he beat me, and, my goodness, the
English don't hit any harder than he does. And then I
had to make my mother cry; there was nothing worse
than that; and then to convince Beaudricourt, who didn't
want to think of anything except adding one more to
his list of sins. Don't think I haven't been afraid. I
was afraid all the time, from the very beginning.

CHARLES. Then how have you done it?

JOAN. Just as I should have done without the fear. That's
all the difficulty there is, Charles. Try it once, and see.
You say: one thing is obvious, I'm frightened, which is
nobody's business but mine, and now on I go. And
on you go. And if you see something ahead which
nothing can overcome . . .

CHARLES. Like Tremouille enjoying one of his rages—

JOAN. Yes, if you like. Or the unshakable English facing
Orleans in their fortress built like rocks. You say: Here
it is—they outnumber us, their walls are as thick as
the length of a giant's arm, their cannons out-thunder
thunder, their arrows out-rain the rain. So be it. I'm
frightened. Now I've realised how frightening it is, on
we go.—And the English are so astonished, they begin
to be frightened themselves, and you get through! You
get through because you think deeper, imagine more,
and get your fear over first. That's the secret of it.

CHARLES. But is it always so successful?

JOAN. Always. As long as you turn and face what frightens you. But the first step has to be yours; He waits for that.

CHARLES (*after a pause*). You think we could try your secret?

JOAN. We have to try it.

CHARLES (*suddenly frightened by his temerity*). Tomorrow, perhaps. By tomorrow I shall have had time to prepare for it.

JOAN. No, Charles; now; you're ready now.

CHARLES. Do you mean that I'm ready to call the Archbishop and La Tremouille? That I'm ready to tell them that I've given you command of the army, and then sit calmly back and watch their faces?

JOAN. Absolutely ready.

CHARLES. I'm scared out of my life.

JOAN. Then the worst is over. One thing is essential: you mustn't be still frightened after you've called them. Are you sure you are as frightened as you possibly can be?

CHARLES (*his hand on his belly*). Oh yes, I agree with you.

JOAN. Wonderful! That's an enormous advantage. When they start to be frightened, you will have got over it already. The whole scheme is to be afraid first, before the battle begins. You'll soon see. I'll call them. (*She calls offstage.*) My Lord Archbishop, M. de la Tremouille! M. le Dauphin wishes to speak to you.

CHARLES (*taken by panic*). Oh dear, I'm so frightened! Goodness, goodness, I'm so frightened.

JOAN. That's it, that's right Charles; more frightened still!

CHARLES (*his teeth chattering*). I can't be more frightened: it's impossible!

54

JOAN. Then we have the victory! God has joined you; He says "Charles is afraid, but still he calls them." In eight hours we shall hold Orleans!

(*Enter the* ARCHBISHOP *and* LA TREMOUILLE, *surprised*.)

ARCHBISHOP. You called us, your Highness?

CHARLES (*suddenly, after a last look at* JOAN). Yes: I've come to a decision, my lord, and it also concerns you, M. de la Tremouille. I am giving the command of my royal army to this Maid here. (*He suddenly shouts*.) If you don't agree, M. de la Tremouille, I must ask you to surrender your sword to me. You are under arrest!

(LA TREMOUILLE *and the* ARCHBISHOP *stand petrified*.)

JOAN (*clapping her hands*). Well done! Now you know how simple it is! Do you see their faces, Charles? Look at them: do look at them! Who is frightened now, Charles?

> *She bursts out laughing;* CHARLES *begins to laugh as well: they rock with laughter, unable to stop; and the* ARCHBISHOP *and* LA TREMOUILLE *seem turned to stone.*

> (JOAN *drops suddenly on to her knees, crying*) Thank you, God!

CHARLES (*also kneeling*). On your knees, M. de la Tremouille, on to your knees! And give us your blessing, Archbishop: no hesitating: give us your blessing! Now that we've all been thoroughly frightened, we must make straight for Orleans!

> LA TREMOUILLE *is on his knees, stupefied by the blow.*

> *The* ARCHBISHOP, *bewildered, mechanically gives his blessing.*

55

PART TWO

WARWICK (*laughing and coming forward with* CAUCHON). In point of fact, that wasn't exactly how it happened. They called a meeting of the Council, and discussed the matter for hours. In the end they agreed to use Joan as a sort of flagpole to nail their colours to: an attractive little mascot, well qualified to charm the general public into letting themselves be killed. The best we could do to restore the balance was to treble the men's drink ration before they went into action, though it had nothing like as good an effect. We started being beaten from that time on, against all the laws of strategy. I know some people have said there was nothing miraculous about that. They maintain that our system of isolated forts around Orleans was ludicrous, and all the enemy had to do was attack: which is what Joan made them agree to try. But that's not true. Sir John Talbot was no fool. He knew his job thoroughly well; as he has proved again and again, both before this regrettable business, and since. His system of fortification was theoretically impregnable. No: we must have the grace to admit there was more in it than that: a strong element of the imponderable—or God, as you might say, my Lord Bishop—which the rules of strategy don't provide for. Without question, it was Joan: singing like a lark in the sky over the heads of your French armies on the march. I am very fond of France, my Lord: which is why I should be most unhappy if we lost her. This lark singing in the sky, while we all take aim to shoot her down: that seems very like France to me. Or at least like the best of her. In her time she has had plenty of fools, rogues and blunderers; but eve'y now and then a lark sings in her sky, and the fools and the rogues can be forgotten. I am very fond of France.

CAUCHON (*gently*). But still you take aim and shoot her down.

WARWICK. A man is a mass of contradictions, my lord Bishop. It isn't unusual in him to kill what he loves. I love animals, but I hunt them, too.

> *He suddenly gets up, looking stern. He raps with his stick on his boot, and makes a sign to* TWO SOLDIERS *who come forward.*

Come along now: the lark has been caught. The cage of Compiègne has shut her in. The singing is over; and Charles and his court are leaving her there, without a second glance. They're going back to their old political methods, now that their little mascot isn't bringing them luck any more.

> *Indeed,* CHARLES, LA TREMOUILLE, *and the* ARCHBISHOP *have slyly got up and edged away from* JOAN, *who is on her knees, praying. She starts up astonished to be alone, and sees* CHARLES *deserting her. The* GUARDS *begin to drag her away.*

CAUCHON. Your king has left you, Joan! There's no reason now to go on defending him. Yesterday we read you the letter he has sent to every town, telling them to say he repudiates you.

JOAN (*after a pause, quietly*). He is my king.

CHARLES (*in a low voice to the* ARCHBISHOP). That letter is going to be thrown in our teeth for a long time yet.

ARCHBISHOP (*also aside*). It had to be, sir: it was absolutely

57

necessary. At this juncture, the cause of France cannot be linked in any way with Joan's.

CAUCHON. Joan: listen carefully, and try to understand what I'm saying. Your king is not our king. A treaty in rightful and due form has made Henry the Sixth of Lancaster King of France and England. Your trial is not a political trial. We are simply trying with all our power and with all our faith to lead a lost sheep back into the fold of our Holy Mother Church. But as men, Joan, we consider ourselves to be faithful subjects of His Majesty King Henry. We have as great and sincere a love of France as you: and because of that we recognise him as our sovereign: so that France can rise up again out of her ruins, dress her wounds, and be free of this appalling, interminable war which has drained all her strength. The useless resistance of the man you call your king, and his absurd pretensions to a throne which isn't his, appear to us to be acts of rebellion and terrorism against a peace which was almost assured. The puppet who you served is not our master, be certain of that.

JOAN. Say what you like, you can't alter the truth. This is the king God gave you. Thin as he is, with his long legs and his big, bony knees.

CHARLES (to the ARCHBISHOP). This is really most disagreeable.

ARCHBISHOP. For a little while we have to have patience; but they mean to hurry through the trial and burn her, and after that we shall not be disturbed. You must surely admit, sir, the English have done us a good turn, making themselves responsible for her arrest and execution. If they hadn't done it, we ourselves should have had to, some day or other. She was becoming impossible!

They withdraw, unnoticed.

58

CAUCHON. We know by many of your answers, insolent though they were, that you're not slow of understanding, Joan. Put yourself for a moment in our place. How can you suppose that we, men with most earnest human convictions, can agree that God has sent you to oppose the cause we defend? How can you think, only because you say voices have spoken to you, that we should believe God to be against us?

JOAN. You will know when we have beaten you.

CAUCHON (*shrugging*). You are answering like a self-willed, obstinate child. Considering the question now as priests and defenders of our Holy Mother Church, have we any better reason to put faith in what you tell us? Do you think you are the first who has heard Voices?

JOAN. No, of course not.

CAUCHON. Neither the first, nor the last, Joan. Now, do you believe that each time a little girl goes to her village priest and says: I have seen some saint, or the Blessed Virgin, I have heard Voices which have told me to do one thing or another—that her priest should believe and encourage her: and how long then would the Church still remain?

JOAN. I don't know.

CAUCHON. You don't know; but you are full of good sense, and that is why I am trying to lead you to reason with me. Have you not been in command in battle, Joan?

JOAN. Yes, I was in command of hundreds of good soldiers who followed me, and believed me.

CAUCHON. You were in command. And if on the morning of some attack one of your soldiers had heard voices persuading him to attack by another gate than the one you had chosen, or not to attack at all, what would you have done?

59

JOAN (*speechless for a moment, before she suddenly bursts out laughing*). My lord Bishop, it's easy to see you're a priest! It's clear you don't know much about our men. They can drink and swear and fight, but they're not ones for hearing Voices!

CAUCHON. A joke is no answer, Joan. But you gave your answer before you spoke, in the second of hesitation when you were held and disarmed by what I said to you. And you see it is true: that the Church militant is an army in a world still overrun by infidels and the powers of evil. The Church owes obedience to our Holy Father the Pope and his bishops, as your soldiers owed obedience to you and your lieutenants. If a soldier says on the morning of attack that Voices have told him not to advance, in yours or any army in the world he would be silenced. And far more brutally than this effort of ours to reason with you.

JOAN (*gathering herself together, on the defensive*). You have a right to hit at me with all your power. And my right is to say No, and go on believing.

CAUCHON. Don't make yourself a prisoner of your own pride, Joan. You can surely see that we have no possible reason, either as men or as priests, to believe that your mission is divinely inspired. You alone have a reason to believe so; encouraged by the fiend who means to damn you, and also, as long as you were useful to them, by those whom you served. You served them; and yet the way they behaved before your capture, and their explicit repudiation since, certainly proves that the most intelligent of them never believed you. No one believes you, Joan, any longer, except the common people, who believe everything, and tomorrow they will believe half a dozen others. You are quite alone.

60

JOAN *makes no reply, sitting small and quiet among them all.*

I beg you not to imagine that your strong will and your stubborn resistance to us is a sign that God is upholding you. The devil has also got intelligence and a tough hide. His mind had the flash of a star among the angels before he rebelled.

JOAN (*after a pause*). I am not intelligent, my lord. I am a peasant girl, the same as any other in my village. But when something is black I cannot say it is white, that is all.

Another pause.

PROMOTER (*suddenly rising up behind her*). What was the sign you gave to the man you are calling your king, to make him trust you with his army?

JOAN. I don't know what you mean: what sign I gave.

PROMOTER. Did you make him sip mandragora, to be a protection against harm?

JOAN. I don't know what you mean by mandragora.

PROMOTER. Your secret has a name, whether it's a potion or a formula, and we mean to know it. What did you give him at Chinon to make him so heroic all of a sudden? A Hebrew name? The devil speaks all languages, but he delights in Hebrew.

JOAN (*smiling*). No, my lord: it has a French name. I gave him courage.

CAUCHON. And so you think that God, or at least the power you believe to be God, took no part in this.

JOAN. He always takes part, my lord Bishop. When a girl speaks two words of good sense and someone listens, there He is. But He is thrifty; when those two words of good sense will do, He isn't likely to throw away a miracle.

61

LADVENU (*quietly*). The answer's a good one, in all humility, my lord: it can't be held against her.

PROMOTER (*with venom, to* JOAN). I see, I see! So you don't believe in such miracles as we are shown in the gospels? You deny what was done by Our Lord Jesus at the marriage of Cana? You deny that He raised Lazarus from the dead?

JOAN. No, my lord. What is written in Holy Scripture was surely done. He changed the water into wine just as easily as He created them. And it was no more extra-ordinary for Him, the Master of life and death, to make Lazarus live again, than for me to thread a needle.

PROMOTER (*yelping*). Listen to that! Listen to that! She says there is no such thing as a miracle!

JOAN. No, my lord. I say that a true miracle is not done with a magic wand or incantation. The gypsies on our village green can do miracles of that sort. The true miracle is done by men themselves, with the mind and the courage which God has given to them.

CAUCHON. Are you measuring the gravity of your words, Joan? You seem to be telling us quite calmly that God's true miracle on earth is man, who is nothing but sin and error, blindness and futility. . . .

JOAN. And strength, too, and courage, and light sometimes when he is deepest in sin. I have seen men during the battles. . . .

LADVENU. My lord, Joan is talking to us in her rough and ready language about things which come instinctively from her heart, which may be wrong but are surely simple and genuine. Her thoughts are not so schooled that she can shape them to our way of argument. Perhaps by pressing her with questions we run the risk of making her say more than she meant, or something different from her belief.

CAUCHON. Brother Ladvenu, we shall try and estimate as fairly as we can what part lack of skill plays in her answers. But our duty is to question her to the last point of doubt. We are not perfectly sure, remember, that our concern now is *only* the question of Joan. So then, Joan, you excuse man all his faults, and think him one of God's greatest miracles, even the only one?

JOAN. Yes, my lord.

PROMOTER (*yelping, beside himself*). It's blasphemy! Man is filth, lust, a nightmare of obscenity!

JOAN. Yes, my lord. He sins; he is evil enough. And then something happens: it may be he is coming out of a brothel, roaring out his bawdy songs in praise of a good time, and suddenly he has thrown himself at the reins of a runaway horse to save some child he has never seen before; his bones broken, he dies at peace.

PROMOTER. But he dies like an animal, without a priest, in the full damnation of sin.

JOAN. No, my lord; he dies in the light which was lighted within him when the world began. He behaved as a man, both in doing evil and doing good, and God created him in that contradiction to make his difficult way.

A storm of indignation from the PRIESTS *when they hear this said. The* INQUISITOR *quietens them, and suddenly rises.*

INQUISITOR (*calmly*). Joan. I have let you speak throughout this trial, with scarcely a question to you. I wanted you to find your way clearly to your position. It has taken some time. The Promoter could see only the Devil, the Bishop only the pride of a young girl intoxicated with success; I waited for something else to show itself. Now it has happened—I represent the Holy Inquisition. My Lord the Bishop told you just now, with great humanity, how his human feelings linked him with the English cause, which he considers just; and how they were confounded by his sentiments as priest and bishop, charged with the defence of our Mother Church. But I have come from the heart of Spain. This is the first time I have been sent to France. I know nothing of either the Armagnac faction, or of the English. It is indifferent to me who shall rule France, whether your prince or Henry of Lancaster. As for that strict discipline of our Mother Church which will not tolerate those who play a lone hand, however well-intentioned, but directs them back into the fold: I'll not say that is indifferent to me; but it is perhaps a secondary task, which the Inquisition leaves to the Bishops and the parish priests. The Holy Inquisition has something higher and more secret to defend than the temporal integrity of the Church. She wrestles on an invisible ground, inwardly, with an enemy only she knows how to detect, of whom only she can estimate the danger. It has been her care sometimes to take up arms against an Emperor; at other times the same solemnity, the same vigilance, the same fixity of purpose have been deployed against some old-apparently inoffensive scholar, or a herdsman buried away in a mountain village, or a young girl. The princes of the earth laugh very heartily to see the Inquisition give itself such endless care, when for them a piece of rope or a sergeant's signature on a death warrant would be enough. The Inquisition lets them laugh. It knows how to recognise the enemy; it knows better than to under-estimate him wherever he may be found. And its enemy is not the devil, not the devil with the cloven hooves, the chastener of troublesome children,

64

whom my lord Promoter sees on every side. His enemy, you yourself spoke his name, when at last you came into the open : his only enemy, is man. Stand up, Joan, and answer me. I am your interrogator now.

> JOAN *rises and turns towards him. He asks in an expressionless voice:*

Are you a Christian?

JOAN. Yes, my lord.

INQUISITOR. You were baptized, and in your earliest years you lived in the shadow of the church whose walls touched the walls of your home. The church bells ruled over your day, your playtime, your work, and your prayers. The emissaries we sent to your village have all come back with the same story : you were a little girl full of piety. Sometimes, instead of playing and running about with other children, though you were not a solemn child, you delighted to play, yet you would slip away into the church, and for a long time you would be there alone, kneeling, not even praying, but gazing at the coloured glass of the window.

JOAN. Yes. I was happy.

INQUISITOR. You had a friend you loved very dearly, a little girl called Haumette.

JOAN. Yes, my lord.

INQUISITOR. And when you made up your mind to leave for Vaucouleurs, already believing that you would never go back, you said goodbye to all your other friends, but you passed her house by.

JOAN. Yes. I was afraid to be too unhappy.

INQUISITOR. But you cared for more than only those you loved most. You cared for old people in sickness, children in poverty. And later on, when you fought in your first battle, you stood among the wounded and cried very bitterly.

JOAN. French blood was being shed; it was hard to bear.

INQUISITOR. Not only because it was French blood. A bully who had captured two English soldiers in a skirmish outside Orleans, knocked one of them down because he didn't move fast enough for him. You jumped off your horse, took the man's head on your knee, wiped the blood from his mouth, and helped him in his dying, calling him your little son, and promising him Heaven.

JOAN. How is it you can know that, my lord?

INQUISITOR. The Holy Inquisition knows everything, Joan. It weighed your human tenderness in the scales before it sent me to judge you.

LADVENU (*rising*). My Lord Inquisitor, I am happy to hear you recalling all these details which until now have been passed over in silence. Yes, indeed, everything we know of Joan since her earliest years has been gentleness, humility, and Christian charity.

INQUISITOR (*turning upon him, suddenly stern*). Silence, Brother Ladvenu! I ask you to remember that I stand here for the Holy Inquisition, alone qualified to make the distinction between Charity, the theological virtue, and the uncommendable, graceless, cloudy drink of the milk of human kindness. (*He passes his eye over them all.*) Ah, my Masters! How quickly your hearts can be melted. The accused has only to be a little girl, looking at you with a pair of wide-open eyes, and with a ha'porth of simple kindness, and you're all ready to fall over yourselves to absolve her. Very good guardians of the faith we have here! I see that the Holy Inquisition has enough to occupy it still: and still so much has to be cut away, cut, cut, always the dead wood to be cut away: and after us, others will go on, still pruning, hacking away without mercy, clearing the ranks of unruliness, so that the forest will be sound from root to branch.

A pause, and then LADVENU *replies.*

LADVENU. Our Saviour also loved with this loving-kindness, my lord. He said: Suffer the little children to come unto me. He put His hand on the shoulder of the woman taken in adultery, and said to her: Go in peace.

INQUISITOR. I tell you to be silent, Brother Ladvenu! Otherwise I shall have to investigate your case as well as Joan's. Lessons from the Gospels are read to the congregations, and we ask the parish priests to explain them. But we have not translated them into the vulgar tongue, or put them into every hand to make of them what they will. How mischievous that would be, to leave untutored souls to let their imaginations play with the texts which only we should interpret. (*He quietens down.*) You are young, Brother Ladvenu, and you have a young man's generosity. But you must not suppose that youth and generosity find grace in the eyes of the faith's defenders. Those are transitory ills which experience will cure. I see that we should have considered your age, and not your learning which I believe is remarkable, before we invited you to join us here. Experience will soon make plain to you that youth, generosity, human tenderness are names of the enemy. At least, I trust it may. Surely you can see, if we were so unwise as to put these words you have spoken into the hands of simple people, they would draw from them a love of Man. And love of Man excludes the love of God.

LADVENU (*quietly*). And yet He chose to become a man . . .

INQUISITOR (*turning suddenly to* CAUCHON, *curtly*). My lord
Bishop, in virtue of your discretionary power as president
of these debates, I ask you to dispense for today with the
collaboration of your young assessor. I shall inform you,
when the sesssion is over, what conclusions will be
entered against him, if needs be. (*He suddenly thunders.*)
Against him or against whomsoever! For no one is of
too great importance to be put out of our care: understand so! I would denounce myself, if God should allow
me to be misled. (*He gravely crosses himself and
ends.*) May He mercifully watch over me!

> *A breath of fear whispers through the tribunal.*
> CAUCHON *says simply, with a gesture of distress to*
> BROTHER LADVENU.

CAUCHON. Leave us, Brother Ladvenu.

LADVENU (*before he moves off*). My lord Inquisitor, I owe
you obedience, as I do my Reverend Lord Bishop. I will
go, saying no more: except that my prayers must be to
our Lord Jesus that He shall lead you to remember the
fragility of your small enemy who faces you now.

INQUISITOR (*not answering until he has gone, and then
speaking quietly*). Small, fragile, tender, pure: and there-
fore formidable. (*He turns to* JOAN *and says in his neutral
tone.*) The first time you heard your Voices you were
not yet fifteen. On that occasion they simply said to you:
" Be a good and sensible child, and go often to church."
In fact you were a happy and contented little girl. And
the unhappiness of France was only old men's talk. And
yet one day you felt you should leave the village.

JOAN. My Voices told me that I must.

INQUISITOR. One day you felt that you must take upon yourself the unhappiness of others around you. And you knew even then everything that would come of it: how glorious your ride would be, how soon it would come to an end, and once your King had been anointed, how you would find yourself where you are now, surrounded and alone, the faggots heaped up in the market place, waiting to be set alight. You know this is——

JOAN. My Voices told me that I should be captured, and then delivered.

INQUISITOR. Delivered! They very well might use that word: and you guessed in what way it might be taken, how ambiguously as a word from heaven. Death is a deliverance, certainly. And you set off all the same, in spite of your father and mother, and in spite of all the grave difficulties ahead of you.

JOAN. Yes, my lord; it had to be. If I had been the daughter of a hundred mothers and a hundred fathers: still it would have had to be.

INQUISITOR. So that you could help your fellow men to keep possession of the soil where they were born, which they fondly imagine belongs to them.

JOAN. Our Lord couldn't want the English to pillage, and kill and overrule us in our own country. When they have gone back across the sea, they can be God's children then in their own land. I shall pick no quarrel with them then.

PROMOTER. Presumption! Pride! Don't you think you would have done better to go on with your sewing and spinning beside your mother?

JOAN. I had something else to do, my lord. There have always been plenty of women to do women's work.

INQUISITOR. When you found yourself in such direct communication with heaven did it never occur to you to consecrate your life to prayer, supplicating that heaven itself should expel the English from France?

JOAN. God likes to see action first, my lord. Prayer is extra. It was simpler to explain to Charles that he ought to attack, and he believed me, and gentle Dunois believed me, too. And so did La Hire and Xantrailles, my fine couple of angry bulls! We had some joyful battles, all of us together. It was good to face every new day with friends, ready to turn on the English, ready to rescue France, ready to——

PROMOTER. Kill, Joan? Ready to kill? And does Our Lord tell us to kill for what we want, as though we had fangs and claws?

(JOAN *does not reply*.)

CAUCHON (*gently*). You loved the war, Joan . . .

JOAN (*simply*). Yes. It is one of the sins which I have most need of God's forgiveness for. Though in the evening I would look across the battlefield and cry to see that the joyous beginning to the morning had gone down in a heap of dead.

PROMOTER. And the next day, you began again?

JOAN. God wished it. While there remained one Englishman in France. It isn't difficult to understand. There was work to be done first, that was all. You are learned, and you think too much. You can't understand the simple things, but the dullest of my soldiers understands them. Isn't that true, La Hire?

LA HIRE *strides forward, in huge armour, gay and alarming.*

LA HIRE. You bet it's true.

70

*Everybody finds himself pushed into the shade: this
one figure is clear. A vague music of the fife is
heard.* JOAN *goes quietly up to him, incredulous, and
touches him with her finger.*

JOAN. La Hire . . .

LA HIRE (*taking up again the comradeship of the battle
mornings*). Well, Miss, we've had the bit of praying we
agreed to have: what's the next thing? Do we take a
bash at them this morning?

JOAN (*throwing herself into his arms*). It is La Hire, my
dear, fat La Hire! You smell so good!

LA HIRE (*embarrassed*). A glass of wine and an onion. It's
my usual morning meal. Excuse me, Miss: I know you
don't like it, but I did my praying beforehand so that
God shouldn't take against my breath. Don't come too
near: I know I stink in a way.

JOAN (*pressed against him*). No: it's good.

LA HIRE. You don't want to make me feel awkward.
Usually you tell me I stink and it's a shame for a
Christian. Usually you say that if the wind carries in that
direction I shall give us away to the goddams, I stink so
much; and we shall ruin our ambush because of me. One
quite small onion and two tots of red wine, no more. Of
course, let's be honest, no water with it.

JOAN. Well, I was a fool if I said so. If an onion has a
right to stink why shouldn't you?

LA HIRE. It's what war does for you. Be a clerk, or a
priest, or a linen draper: no smell. But be a captain,
you're bound to sweat. As for washing, up in the line: a
man doesn't see the interest in it. There was no need to
add the onion, I suppose: I ought to do with a bit of
garlic sausage like the other fellows: it's better behaved

71

when you come to conversation. But, look here, you wouldn't call it a sin, would you, eating the onion?

JOAN (*smiling*). No, La Hire: not a sin.

LA HIRE. You never know with you, you know.

JOAN. Have I pestered you with sins, La Hire? I was silly to tease you so much: it's odd, but there you are, a great bear smelling of sweat and onions and red wine, and you kill, and swear, and think of nothing except the girls. . . .

LA HIRE (*very astonished*). Who, me?

JOAN. You. Yes. Look astonished, you old rogue. And yet you shine in the hand of God as bright as a new penny.

LA HIRE. Is that a fact? I should have thought I'd bitched my chance of paradise years ago. But you think if I keep on praying as arranged, a bit every day, I might still get there?

JOAN. They're expecting you. I know that God's paradise must be full of ruffians like you.

LA HIRE. Is that a fact? It would make all the difference to feel that there were a few kindred spirits around. I wasn't much looking forward to being in a crowd of saints and bishops looking like Heaven's village idiot.

JOAN (*gaily thumping him*). Great Jackass! Of course Heaven's full of dunces. Hasn't our Lord said so? It may even be they're the only ones who get in: the others have had so many brains to sin with, they never get past the door.

LA HIRE (*uneasily*). You don't think, between ourselves, we'll get bored to death, do you, always on our best behaviour? Any fighting at all, do you imagine?

JOAN. All the day long.

LA HIRE (*respectfully*). Wait, now. Only when God isn't looking at us.

JOAN. But He's looking at you all the time, crackpot! He sees everything. And what's more, He is going to enjoy watching you at it. "Go it, La Hire," He'll say: "Bash the stuffing out of old Xantraille! Pitch into him, now! Show him what you're made of!"

LA HIRE. Is that a fact?

JOAN. Not in those words perhaps, but in His own way.

LA HIRE. By God Almighty. (*Enthusiastically.*)

JOAN (*suddenly stern*). La Hire!

LA HIRE (*hanging his head*). Sorry, miss.

JOAN (*pitilessly*). If you swear He will throw you out.

LA HIRE (*stammering*). I was feeling pleased, you see: had to thank Him somehow.

JOAN. So He thought. But don't do it again! We've talked quite enough for one morning. Let's get up on horseback and take a look at the day.

LA HIRE. It's dead country this morning. Not a soul to see. *They ride imaginary horses side by side.*

JOAN. Look, we've got France all to ourselves—shall we ever see the world to better advantage? Here on horseback side by side: this is how it will be, La Hire, when the English have gone. Smell the wet grass, La Hire, isn't this why men go fighting? To ride out together smelling the world when the light of day is just beginning to discover it.

LA HIRE. So anyone can who likes to take a walk in his garden.

JOAN. No. I think death has to be somewhere near before God will show us the world like this.

LA HIRE. Suppose we should meet some English, who might also be liking the good smells of the morning?

JOAN. We attack them, we smite them, and send them flying. That's what we're here for!

A little pause.

(*She suddenly cries.*) Stop!

They draw in their horses.

There are three English over there. They've seen us. They're running away! No! Now they've turned back again: they've seen there are only two of us. They're attacking. You're not afraid, La Hire? No use counting on me; I'm only a girl, and I've got no sword. Will you fight them alone?

LA HIRE (*brandishing his sword with a delighted roar*). Hell, yes, by God I will! (*Shouting to the sky as he charges.*) I didn't say anything, God, I didn't say anything. Pay no attention . . .

He charges into the middle of the Tribunal: they scatter as he swings his sword to left and right. He disappears still fighting.

JOAN. He didn't say anything, God. He didn't say anything! He is as good as a French loaf. So all my soldiers are, though they kill, and loot, and swear: good as your wolves are, God, whom you created innocent. I will answer for all of them!

JOAN is deep in prayer. The Tribunal has re-formed round her: the light has come back. JOAN raises her head, sees them, seems to shake herself free of a dream.

La Hire and Xantrailles! Oh, we're not at the end of things yet. You can be sure they will come and deliver me with two or three or four hundred men . . .

74

CAUCHON (*quietly*). They came, Joan: right up to the gates of Rouen to find out how many of the English were in the town, and then they went away again.

JOAN (*dashed*). Oh, they went away? Without fighting? (*A silence; she looks up.*) Why, they have gone to find reinforcements, of course. I myself taught them, it is no good to attack willynilly, as they did at Agincourt.

CAUCHON. They withdrew to the South of the Loire; Charles is down there, disbanding his armies. He is tired of the war, and if he can he will make a treaty, to secure at least his own small portion of France. They will never come back again, Joan.

JOAN. That isn't true! La Hire will come back, even if he hasn't a chance.

CAUCHON. La Hire is only the captain of an army of mercenaries, who sold himself and his men to another Prince as soon as he found that yours was out to make peace. He is marching at this moment towards Germany, to find another country to plunder; simply that.

JOAN. It isn't true!

CAUCHON (*rising*). Have I ever lied to you, Joan? It is true. Then why will you sacrifice yourself to defend those who have deserted you? The only men on earth who are trying to save you—paradoxical though it may seem—are ourselves, your old enemies and now your judges. Recant, Joan: your resistance helps no-one now; your friends are betraying you. Return to the arms of your Mother Church. Humble yourself, she will lift you up again. I am convinced that deep in your heart you have never ceased to be one of her daughters.

JOAN. Yes, I am a daughter of the Church!

CAUCHON. Then give yourself into the care of your mother, Joan, without question. She will weigh your burden of error, and so release you from the anguish of judging it for yourself. You needn't think of anything any more: you will do your penance, whether it be heavy or light, and at last you will be at peace. Surely you have a great need of peace.

JOAN (*after a pause*). In what concerns the Faith, I trust myself to the Church. But what I have done I shall never wish to undo.

(*A stir among the priests. The* INQUISITOR *breaks in.*)

INQUISITOR. Do you hear, my masters? Do you see Man raising up his head, like a serpent ready to strike us dead? Do you understand now what it is you have to judge? These heavenly voices have deafened you as well as the girl, on my word they have! You have been labouring to discover what devil has been behind her actions. Would it were only a question of the devil. His trial would soon be over. The devil speaks our language. In his time he was an angel, and we understand him. The sum of his blasphemies, his insults, even his hatred of God, is an act of faith. But man, calm and transparent as he seems, frightens me infinitely more. Look at him: in chains, disarmed, deserted, no longer sure even in himself (isn't that so, Joan?) that the voices which have been silent for so long have ever truly spoken. Does he throw himself down, supplicating God to hold him again in His hand? Does he at least implore his Voices to come back and give light to his path? No. He turns away, suffers the torture, suffers humiliation and beating, suffers like a dumb animal, while his eyes fasten on the invincible image of himself; (*he thunders*) himself, his only true God! That is what I fear! And he replies—repeat it, Joan; you are longing to say it again: " But what I have done . . . "

JOAN (*quietly*) . . . I shall never wish to undo.

INQUISITOR (*repeats*). ' But what I have done I shall never wish to undo! '. You hear those words? And you will hear them said on the scaffold, at the stake, in the torture chamber, wherever they come to suffer for the errors they commit. And centuries hence they will be saying it; the hunting down of Man will go on endlessly. However powerful we become one day in one shape or another, however inexorably the Idea shall dominate the world, however rigorous, precise and subtle its organisation and its police, there will always be a man who has escaped, a man to hunt, who will presently be caught, presently be killed: a man who, even so, will humiliate the Idea at the highest point of its Power, simply because he will say " No " without lowering his eyes. (*He hisses through his teeth, looking at* JOAN *with hatred.*) An insolent breed! (*He turns again towards the Tribunal.*) Do you need to question her any more? Do you need to ask her why she threw herself from the height of the tower where she was imprisoned, whether to escape, or to destroy herself against the commandments of God? Why she has left her father and mother, put on the clothes of a man, and wears them still, against the commandments of the Church? She will give you the same reply, the reply of Man: What I have done, I have done. It is mine, and my doing. No-one can take it from me; no-one can make me disown it. All that you can do is kill me, to make me cry out no matter what under the torture, but make me say " Yes ", you cannot do. (*He cries to them.*) Ah well: by some means or other he must be taught to say Yes, whatever it may cost the world. As long as one man remains who will not be broken, the Idea, even if it dominates and pervades all the rest of mankind, will be in danger of perishing. That is why I require Joan's excommunication, her rejection from the bosom of the Church and that she should be given over to the secular arm for punishment. (*He adds neutrally, reciting a formula.*) Beseeching it nevertheless to limit its sentence on this side of death and the mutilation of the limbs. (*He turns to* JOAN.) This will be a paltry victory against you, Joan, but at least it will silence you. And, up to now, we have not thought of a better. (*He sits down again in silence.*)

CAUCHON (*gently*). My Lord Inquisitor is the first to ask for your excommunication, Joan. In a moment I am afraid my Lord Promoter will ask for the same thing. Each one of us will speak his mind and then I shall have to give my decision. Before lopping the dead branch, which you have become, and casting it far from her, your Holy Mother Church, to whom the one lost sheep is more dear than all the others, remember that, entreats you now for the last time.

　　CAUCHON *makes a sign, and a man comes forward.* Do you know this man, Joan?
　　She turns to look and gives a little shudder of fear.
It is the master hangman of Rouen. In a short while from now you will belong to him, unless you give your soul into our keeping so that we can save it. Is the stake ready, Master Hangman?

HANGMAN. Quite ready, my lord. Higher than the regulation stake, such was the orders: so that the girl can be got a good view of from all sides. The nuisance of it for her is that I shan't be able to help her at all, she will be too high up.

78

CAUCHON. What do you call helping her, Master Hangman?

HANGMAN. A trick of the trade, my lord: it's the custom, when there aren't any special instructions. You wait till the first flames get up, and then I climb up behind, under cover of the smoke, and strangle the party. Then it's only the corpse that burns, and it isn't so bad. But with the instructions I've had, it's too high, and I won't be able to get up there. (*He adds simply*) So, naturally, it will take longer.

CAUCHON. Do you hear that, Joan?

JOAN (*softly*). Yes.

CAUCHON. I am going to offer you once more the hand of your Mother, the great hand which opens towards you to take you back and save you. But the delay can't be for long. You hear the noise outside, as though the sea had come up to the door? That is the sound of the crowd, who already have been waiting for you since daybreak. They came early to get good places: and there they are still, eating the food they brought with them, grumbling at their children, joking and singing, and asking the soldiers how long it will be before things begin to happen. They are not bad people. They are the same men and women who would have cheered you if you had captured Rouen. But things have turned out differently, that's all, and so instead they come to see you burned. As nothing very much ever happens to them, they make their adventures out of the triumphs or the deaths of the world's great ones. You will have to forgive them, Joan. All their lives long they pay dearly for being the common people; they deserve these little distractions.

JOAN (*quietly*). I do forgive them. And I forgive you, as well, my lord.

PROMOTER. Appalling, abominable pride! My lord the Bishop troubles to talk to you like a father, in the hope of saving your miserable soul, and you have the effrontery to say that you forgive him!

JOAN. My lord talks to me gently, but I don't know whether it is to save me or to overthrow me. And since in a little while he will have to burn me anyway, I forgive him.

CAUCHON. Joan: try to understand that there is something absurd in your refusal. You are not an unbeliever. The God you claim as your own is ours also. And we are, in fact, those whom God has ordained to guide you, through the apostle Peter upon whom His Church is built. God did not say to His creatures: You will understand My will from Me. He said " Thou art Peter, and upon this rock I will build My church . . . and its priests will be your shepherds . . . ". Do you think us unworthy priests, Joan?

JOAN (*quietly*). No.

CAUCHON. Then why will you not do as God has said? Why will you not resign your fault to the Church, as you did when you were a small girl, at home in your village? Has your faith so changed?

JOAN. (*crying out in anguish*). I want to submit to the Church. I want to receive the Holy Sacrament, but you won't let me!

CAUCHON. We will give it to you after your confession, and when your penance has begun; we only wait for you to say ' Yes '. You are brave, we know that indeed: but your flesh is still frail: you are surely afraid of dying?

JOAN (*quietly*). Yes. I'm afraid. But what else can I do?

CAUCHON. I think well enough of you, Joan, to know that fear in itself is not enough to make you draw back. But you should have another, greater fear: the fear of being deceived, and of laying yourself open to eternal damnation. Now, what risk do you run, even if your voices are from God, if you perform the act of submission to the priests of His church? If we do not believe in your Voices, and if nevertheless God has really spoken to you, then it is we who have committed the monstrous sin of ignorance, presumption and pride, and we who will have to make expiation through all eternity. We will take this risk for you, Joan, and you risk nothing. Say to us: ' I submit to you ', say simply ' Yes ', and you will be at peace, blameless, and safe in your redemption.

JOAN (*suddenly exhausted*). Why will you torture me so gently, my lord? I would far rather you beat me.

CAUCHON (*smiling*). If I beat you, Joan, I should only add to your pride: your pride which wishes to see you persecuted and killed. I reason with you because God gifted you with reason and good sense. I beseech you, because I know you have gentle feeling. I am an old man, Joan; I have no more ambitions in this world, and, like each of us here, I have put many to death in defence of the Church, as you have put many to death in defence of your Voices. It is enough. I am tired. I wish to die without adding to those deaths the death of a little girl. Help me.

JOAN (*after a pause*). What do I have to say?

CAUCHON. First of all you must understand that by insisting that God sent you, you no longer help anything or anyone. It is only playing into the hand of the English and the Executioner. Your king himself has declared in his letters that he doesn't in any way wish to owe the

81

possession of his crown to a divine intervention of which you were the instrument.

JOAN *turns towards* CHARLES *in distress.*

CHARLES. Put yourself in my place, Joan! If there had to be a miracle to crown me King of France, it means I wasn't naturally king at all. It means I wasn't the true son of my father, or else my coronation would have followed of its own accord. All the other kings in my family have been crowned without needing a miracle. Divine help is all very well in its way, but suspect. And it's even more suspect when it stops. Since that unhappy Paris business, we've been beaten at every step; and then you let yourself be captured at Compiegne. They've got a little verdict up their sleeve for you, to denounce you as a witch, a heretic, the devil's intermediary, all in one. I prefer people to think you were never sent by anyone, God or devil. In that way, God has neither helped me, nor thrown me over. I won because I was the strongest at the time; I am being beaten now because I am the weakest, for the moment. That is healthy politics, if you understand?

JOAN (*softly*). Yes, I understand.

CAUCHON. I'm thankful to see you're wiser at last. We have put so many questions to you, you became confused. I am going to ask you three more, three essential ones. If you answer "Yes" three times, we shall all of us be saved, you who are going to die, and we who are putting you to death.

JOAN (*quietly, after a pause*). Ask them. I will see whether I can answer them.

CAUCHON. The first question is the really important one. If you answer "yes", the other answers will take care of themselves. Listen carefully, weighing each word:

Do you humbly put yourself into the hands of the Holy Apostolic Church of Rome; of our Holy Father the Pope and his bishops, that they shall estimate your deeds and judge you? Do you surrender yourself entirely and undoubtedly, and do you ask to be received again into the bosom of the Church? " It is enough for you to answer " yes ".

> JOAN *after a pause, looks around her without moving. At last she speaks.*

JOAN. Yes, but . . .

INQUISITOR (*in a level voice*). With no " but ".

JOAN. I do not wish to be made to deny what my Voices have said to me. I do not wish to be made to bear witness against my king, or to say anything which will dim the glory of his coronation which is his, irrevocably, now and for ever.

> *The* INQUISITOR *shrugs his shoulders.*

INQUISITOR. Such is the voice of man. There is only one way of bringing him to silence.

CAUCHON (*becoming angry*). Joan, Joan, Joan, are you mad? Do you not see this man in red who is waiting for you? Realise, understand, this is my last effort to save you, after this there is nothing more I can do. The Church still wishes to believe that you are one of her daughters. She has weighed with care the form her question should take, to help you on the path, and you cavil and try to bargain. There is no bargaining with your Mother, you impudent girl! You should beg her on your knees to wrap you in her cloak of love and protect you. Our Lord suffered far more than you in the humiliation and injustice of His Passion. Did He bargain or cavil when He came to die for you? Your suffering bears no comparison with His: scourged, mocked, spat upon: crowned with thorns, and nailed in a long agony between two thieves; you can never hope to rival His suffering! And He asks, through us, only one thing of you, that you submit to the judgment of His Church, and you hesitate.

JOAN (*after a pause, tears in her eyes*). Forgive me, my lord. I hadn't thought that Our Saviour might wish it. It is true that He has surely suffered more than I. (*A short pause, again, and she says*) I submit.

CAUCHON. Do you humbly and without any restriction supplicate the Holy Catholic Church to receive you again into her bosom, and do you defer to her judgment?

JOAN. I humbly supplicate my Mother Church to receive me again into her bosom, and I surrender myself to her judgment.

CAUCHON (*with a sigh of relief*). Good, Joan; well done. The rest will be simple enough now. Do you promise never again to take up arms?

JOAN. There is still work to be done . . .

CAUCHON. The work, as you call it, will be done by others. Don't be foolish, Joan. You are in chains, a prisoner, and in great danger of being burned. So whether you say yes or no the work will not be done by you. Your part is played out. The English have you in their grasp, and they'll not let you fight again. You said to us just now that when a girl has two words of good sense God is there performing His miracle. If God is protecting you, this is the time for Him to bring you the two words of good sense. So you promise never again to take up arms?

JOAN (*groaning*). But if my King still needs me?

84

CHARLES (*hastily*). Oh, goodness me! If it's me you're thinking about you can say yes at once. I don't need you any more.

JOAN (*heavily*). Then, yes; yes.

CAUCHON. Do you promise never to wear again these man's clothes, which is contrary to all the rules of decency and Christian modesty?

JOAN (*tired of the question*). You have asked me that ten times. The clothes are nothing. My Voices told me to wear them.

PROMOTER. The devil told you! Who except the devil would incite a girl to overthrow decency?

JOAN (*quietly*). Common sense, my lord.

PROMOTER (*sneering*). Common sense? Common sense is your strong card! Are breeches on a girl common sense?

JOAN. Of course, my lord. I had to ride horseback with the soldiers: I had to wear what they wore so that they wouldn't think of me as a girl, but as a soldier like themselves.

PROMOTER. A worthless reply! A girl who isn't damned to begin with wouldn't wish to ride with the soldiers!

CAUCHON. Even though it may be that these clothes had their purpose during the war, why do you still refuse to dress as a woman? The fighting's over, you are in our hands; yet you still refuse.

JOAN. It is necessary.

CAUCHON. Why?

JOAN (*hesitating for a moment, blushing*). If I were in a Church prison, I wouldn't refuse then.

PROMOTER. You hear this nonsense, my lord? What hair splitting: what deliberate prevarication! Why should

85

she agree to modesty in a Church prison, and not where she is? I don't understand it, and I don't wish to!

JOAN (*smiling sadly*). And yet it is very easy to understand, my lord. You don't have to be very wise to see it.

PROMOTER. It is very easy to understand, and I don't understand because I'm a fool, I suppose? Will you note that, my lord? She insults me, in the exercise of my public office. She treats her indecency as something to glory in, boasts of it, in fact. Takes a gross delight in it, I've no doubt! If she submits to the Church, as she apparently wants to, I may have to give up my chief accusation of heresy; but as long as she refuses to put off this diabolical dress, I shall persist in my charge of witchcraft, even though pressure is put upon me by the conspiracy to shield her which I see presides over this debate. I shall appeal, if necessary, to the Council of Basle! The devil is in this, my lord, the devil is in it! I can feel his terrible presence! He it is who is making her refuse to give up these clothes of immodesty and vice, no doubt of that.

JOAN. Put me in a Church prison, and I shall give them up.

PROMOTER. You shall not make your bargains with the Church: my lord has already told you so. You will give up this dress altogether, or you will be condemned as a witch and burnt!

CAUCHON. If you accept the principle, Joan, why don't you wish to obey us now, in the prison where you are?

JOAN. I'm not alone there.

PROMOTER. Well? you're not alone there. Well? What of that?

JOAN. The English soldiers are on guard in the cell, all through the day, and through the night.

PROMOTER. Well? (*A pause.*) Do you mean to go on? Your powers of invention have failed you already, is that it? I should have thought the devil was more ingenious! You feel that you've been caught out, my girl, and it makes you blush.

CAUCHON (*quietly*). You must answer him, Joan. I think I understand but it must be you who tells us so.

JOAN (*after a moment of hesitation*). The nights are long, my lord. I am in chains. I do my best to keep awake, but sleep sometimes is too strong for me. (*She stops*).

PROMOTER (*more and more obtuse*). Well, what then? The nights are long, you are in chains, you want to sleep. What then?

JOAN (*quietly*). I can defend myself better if I wear these clothes.

CAUCHON (*heavily*). Has this been so all the time of the trial?

JOAN. Ever since I was captured, my lord, each night; and when you send me back there in the evening, it begins again. I've got into the way of not sleeping now, which is why my answers are so sleepy and muddled when I'm brought before you in the mornings. But each night seems longer; and the soldiers are strong, and full of tricks. I should as soon wear a woman's dress on the battlefield.

CAUCHON. Why don't you call the officer, and he would defend you?

JOAN (*after a pause*). They told me they would be hanged if I called for help.

WARWICK (*to* CAUCHON). Incredible. I never heard of such a thing! Quite possible in the French army. But in the English army, no, quite ridiculous. I shall inquire into this.

CAUCHON. If you would return, Joan, back to your Mother the Church who is waiting for you: promise to change from these clothes to the dress of a girl: the Church from now on would see you had no such fears.

JOAN. Then I do promise.

CAUCHON (*giving a deep sigh*). Good. Thank you, Joan, you have helped me. I was afraid for a time we should have no power to save you. We shall read your promise to adjure your sins: the document is all ready, you have only to sign it.

JOAN. I don't know how to write.

CAUCHON. You will make a cross. My lord Inquisitor, allow me to recall Brother Ladvenu so that he may read this to the prisoner. It is Brother Ladvenu who is responsible, at my request, for drawing up this paper. And, moreover, we have all to be here now, to pronounce sentence, now that Joan has returned to us. (*He leans towards him.*) You should be gratified, my lord: Man has said ' yes '.

INQUISITOR (*a pallid smile on his thin lips*). I am waiting until the conclusion; until the conclusion.

    CAUCHON *calls to the* GUARD.

CAUCHON. Recall Brother Ladvenu!

PROMOTER (*whispering*). My lord Inquisitor, you won't allow them to do this?

INQUISITOR (*with a vague gesture*). If she has said ' yes ' . . .

PROMOTER. My lord Bishop has conducted the enquiry

with an indulgence towards the girl which I can't begin to understand! And yet I have reliable information that he feeds well from the English manger. Does he feed even more rapaciously from the French? That is what I ask myself.

INQUISITOR (*smiling*). It is not what I ask myself, my lord Promoter. It is not of eating, well or better, that I am thinking, but of something graver. (*He falls on to his knees, oblivious of all around him.*) O Lord! It has pleased You to grant that Man should humble himself at the eleventh hour in the person of this young girl. It has been Your will that this time he shall say ' Yes '. But why has it also pleased You to let an evident and earthly tenderness be born in the heart of this old man who was judging her? Will you never grant, O Lord, that this world should be unburdened of every trace of humanity, so that at last we may in peace consecrate it to Thy glory alone?

BROTHER LADVENU *has come forward.*

CAUCHON. She is saved, Brother Ladvenu, Joan is saved. She has agreed to return to us, and to Holy Mother Church. Read her the act of Abjuration, and she will sign it.

LADVENU. Thank you, Joan. I was praying for you, I prayed that this might be possible. (*He reads*) ' I, Joan, known as the Maid, confess to having sinned, by pride, obstinacy, and wrong-doing, in pretending to receive revelation from Our Lord God, Father of all Men, through the means of His angels and His blessed Saints. I confess to having blasphemed by wearing immodest clothing, contrary to the ruling of our Holy Mother Church; and to having, by persuasion, incited men to kill one another. I forswear and abjure all these

89

sins; I vow upon the Holy Gospels no more to wear these clothes or to bear arms. I promise to surrender myself in humility to our Holy Mother Church, and to our Holy Father the Pope of Rome, and to his Bishops, that they shall weigh and estimate my sins and wickedness. I beseech the Church to receive me again into her bosom; and I declare myself ready to suffer the sentence which it will please her to inflict upon me. In token of which I have signed my name to this Act of Abjuration which I profess I have understood.'

JOAN (*who seems now like a shy and awkward girl*). Do I make a circle or a cross? I can't write my name.

LADVENU. I will guide your hand. (*He helps her to sign.*)

CAUCHON. There; it is done, Joan; and the Church rejoices to see her daughter safely returned: and you know she rejoices more for the one lost sheep than for the ninety-and-nine safely enfolded. Your soul is saved, and your body will not be delivered up to the executioner. We condemn you only, through the mercy and the grace of God, to live the rest of your days a prisoner, in penitence of these errors, eating the bread of sorrow, drinking the water of anguish, so that in solitary contemplation you may repent; and by these means we shall admit you free of the danger of excommunication into which you were fallen. You may go in peace. (*He makes the sign of the cross over her.*) Take her away.

The SOLDIERS *lead* JOAN *away.*

The assembly breaks up into groups, conversing among themselves.

WARWICK (*coming up to* CAUCHON). Good enough, my lord; good enough. I was wondering for a moment or so what irresponsible whim was urging you to save the girl, and whether you hadn't a slight inclination to betray your king.

CAUCHON. Which king, my lord?

WARWICK (*with a touch of frigidity*). I said your king. I imagine you have only one? Yes; very uncertain for a time whether His Majesty was going to get his money's worth, owing to this fancy of yours. But then, when I thought about it, I could see this method would discredit young Charles equally well, without the disadvantages of martyrdom, which are unpredictable, when you think of the sort of sentimental reactions we get from the public. The resolute, unshakable girl, tied to the stake and burning in the flames, would have seemed, even so, something of a triumph for the French cause. This admission of guilt, on the other hand, is properly disgraceful. Perfect.

The CHARACTERS *move away.*

The lighting changes.

JOAN *is brought on by a* GUARD. AGNES SOREL *and* QUEEN YOLANDE *slip in beside her.*

AGNES (*coming forward*). Joan, Joan, my dear; we're so very happy it has all turned out well for you. Congratulations!

YOLANDE. Dying is quite useless, my little Joan: and whatever we do in life should have a use of some kind. People may have different opinions about the way my life has been lived, but at least I've never done anything absolutely useless.

AGNES. It was all so very stupid. Usually I adore political trials, and I particularly begged Charles to get me a seat; to watch someone fighting for his life is desperately exciting, as a rule. But really I didn't feel in the least happy when I was there. All the time I kept saying to myself: This is so very stupid: this poor little tomboy: she is going to get herself killed, and all for nothing. (*She takes* CHARLES' *arm*). Being alive is much better, you know, in every way.

CHARLES. Yes, of course it is; and when you practically ruined your chances, just because of me—well, I was very touched, naturally, but I didn't know how to make you understand that you were getting everything quite wrong. In the first place, as you might expect, I had taken the precaution to disown you, on the advice of that old fox of an Archbishop; but, more than that, I don't like people being devoted to me. I don't like being loved. It creates obligations, and obligations are detestable.

> JOAN *does not look at them; she hears their prattle without seeming to hear it. Then suddenly she speaks quietly.*

JOAN. Take care of Charles. I hope he keeps his courage.

AGNES. Of course he will; why shouldn't he? My way with him is not so different from yours. I don't want him to be a poor little king who is always being beaten, any more than you do; and you shall see, I shall make our Charles a great King yet, and without getting myself burnt either. (*She adds in a low voice.*) I suppose it may be rather disillusioning to say so, Joan (though, of course, the two sexes are presumably what God wanted): but I do seem to get as much out of CHARLES by my little campaigns in the bedroom as ever you did with swords and angels.

JOAN (*murmuring*). Poor Charles . . .

AGNES. Why poor? He is perfectly happy, like all egoists:

and one of these days he is going to be a great king into the bargain.

YOLANDE. We shall see that done, Joan: not your way, but ours, and effectively enough.

AGNES (*with a gesture to the little* QUEEN). Even her little Majesty will help. She has just given him a second son. It is all she can do, but she does it very well. So if the first son dies there is no feverish worry. The succession is assured. You can be quite happy, Joan, that you're leaving everything in good order at the Court of France.

CHARLES (*after a sneeze*). Are you coming, my dear? This prison atmosphere is deadly, so damp it would really be healthier to sit in the river. Goodbye, Joan, for the moment; we'll come and visit you from time to time.

JOAN. Goodbye, Charles.

CHARLES. Goodbye, goodbye . . . I might say, if ever you come back to Court, you will have to call me Sire, like anybody else. I've seen to that, since my coronation. Even La Tremouille does it. It's a great victory.

They go off, rustling their robes.

JOAN (*murmuring*). Goodbye, Sire. I am glad I got you that privilege at least.

The light changes again, as the GUARD *leads her to a three-legged stool; she is alone now in her cell.*

Blessed St Michael, blessed ladies Catherine and Margaret, are you never going to come again and speak to me? Why have you left me alone since the English captured me? You were there to see me safely to victory: but it's now, in the suffering time, that I need you most. I know it would be too simple, too easy, if God always held me by the hand: where would the merit be? I know

He took my hand at the beginning because I was still too small to be alone, and later He thought I could make my own way. But I am not very big yet, God. It was very difficult to follow clearly everything the Bishop said to me. With the Canon it was easy: I could see where he was wrong, and where he was wicked, and I was ready to give him any answer which would make him furious. But the Bishop spoke so gently, and it often seemed to me he was right. Are you sure that you meant that, God? Did you mean me to feel so afraid of suffering, when the man said he would have no chance to strangle me before the flames could reach me? Are you sure that you want me to live? (*A pause. She seems to be waiting for an answer, her eyes on the sky.*) No word for me? I shall have to answer that question for myself, as well. (*A pause. She nods.*) Perhaps I am only proud and self-willed after all? Perhaps after all, I did imagine everything?

> *Another pause. She suddenly bursts into tears, her head on the stool.* WARWICK *comes quickly on to the stage, preceded by a* GUARD *who leaves them at once.* WARWICK *stops, and looks at* JOAN, *surprised.*

WARWICK. Are you crying?

JOAN. Yes, my lord.

WARWICK. And I came here to congratulate you! That was a very happy solution to it all, I thought, the outcome of the trial, very. I told Cauchon, I was delighted you managed to avoid an execution. Quite apart from my own personal sympathy for you, the suffering is really frightful, you know, and quite useless, and most unpleasant to watch. I'm perfectly convinced you've done right to steer clear of martyrdom; better for us all. I congratulate you most sincerely. It was astonishing, considering the peasant stock you come from, that you should behave with such distinction. A gentleman is always ready, when he must, to die for his honour or his king, but it's only the riff-raff who get themselves killed for nothing. And then I was very entertained to see you queen the Inquisitor's pawn. A sinister character, that Inquisitor fellow! I detest intellectuals more than anybody. These fleshless people, what unpleasant fossils they are—Are you really a virgin?

JOAN. Yes.

WARWICK. Well, yes, of course you are. No woman would have spoken quite in the way you did. My fiancée in England, who's a very innocent girl, reasons exactly like a boy herself, and, like you, there's no gainsaying her. There's an Indian proverb—I don't know whether you may have heard it—which says it takes a virgin to walk on water. (*He gives a little laugh.*) We shall see how long she manages that, once she becomes Lady Warwick! Being a virgin is a state of grace. We adore them, and revere them, and yet, the sad thing is, as soon as we meet one we're in the greatest possible hurry to make a woman of her: and we expect the miracle to go on as if nothing had happened. Madmen! Just as soon as ever this campaign is over—it won't be long now, I hope: your little Charles is tottering to a fall—but as soon as it is, back I go to England, to do that very same idiotic thing. Warwick Castle is a very beautiful place, a bit big, a bit severe, but very beautiful. I breed superb horses—and my fiancée rides rather well, not as well as you do, but rather well. So she ought to be very happy there. We shall go fox-hunting, of course, and entertain fairly lavishly from time to time. I'm only sorry the circumstances make it so difficult to invite you over. (*An awkward pause.*) Well, there it is, I thought I'd pay you

95

this visit, rather like shaking hands after a match, if you know what I mean. I hope I haven't disturbed you. Are my men behaving themselves now?

JOAN. Yes.

WARWICK. I should think they will certainly transfer you to a Church prison. But in any case, until they do, if there's any sign of a lapse, don't hesitate to report it to me. I'll have the blackguard hung. It's not really possible to have a whole army of gentlemen, but we can try. (*He bows.*) Madam.

He starts to go. JOAN *calls him back.*

JOAN. My lord!

WARWICK (*returning*). Yes?

JOAN (*without looking at him*). It would have been better, wouldn't it, if I had been burned?

WARWICK. I told you, for His Majesty's Government, the admission of guilt was just as good.

JOAN. But for me?

WARWICK. Unprofitable suffering. An ugly business. No, really, it wouldn't have been better. It would have been, as I told you just now, slightly plebeian, and ill-bred, and more than slightly stupid, to insist on dying just to embarrass everybody and make a demonstration.

JOAN (*as though to herself*). But I am ill-bred, I am stupid. And then, remember, my lord, my life isn't prepared and perfected like yours, running so orderly and smoothly between war, hunting, and your beautiful bride waiting for you in England. What is left of me when I am not Joan any longer?

WARWICK. Life isn't going to be very gay for you, I agree, not at first anyway. But things will adjust themselves in time, I don't think you need have any doubt of that

JOAN. But I don't want things to adjust themselves. I don't want to live through however long this ' in time ' of yours will be. (*She gets up like a sleepwalker, and stares blindly ahead*.) Do you see Joan after living through it, when things have adjusted themselves: Joan, set free, perhaps, and vegetating at the French Court on her small pension?

WARWICK (*impatient*). My dear girl, I can tell you, in six months there won't be a French Court!

JOAN (*almost laughing, though sadly*). Joan accepting everything, Joan fat and complacent, Joan doing nothing but eat. Can you see me painted and powdered, trying to look fashionable, getting entangled in her skirts, fussing over her little dog, or trailing a man at her heels: who knows, perhaps with a husband?

WARWICK. Why not? Everything has to come to an end sometime. I'm going to be married myself.

JOAN (*suddenly cries out in another voice*). But I don't want everything to come to an end! Or at least not an end like that, an end which is no end at all. Blessed St. Michael: St. Margaret: St. Catherine! You may be silent now, but I wasn't born until you first spoke to me, that day in the fields: my life truly began when I did what you told me to do, riding horseback with a sword in my hand. And that is Joan, and no other one. Certainly not one sitting placid in her convent, pasty-faced and going to pieces in comfort: continuing to live as a tolerable habit: set free, they would call it! You kept yourself silent, God, while all the priests were trying to speak at once, and everything became a confusion of words. But You told St. Michael to make it clear to me in the very beginning, that when You're silent You have then the most certain trust in us. It is the time when You let us take on everything alone. (*She draws herself up.*) Well, I take it on, O

97

God: I take it upon myself! I give Joan back to You: true to what she is, now and forever! Call your soldiers, Warwick; call them, call them, quickly now: for I tell you I withdraw my admission of guilt: I take back my promises: they can pile their faggots, and set up their stake: they can have their holiday after all!

WARWICK (*bored*). Now for God's sake don't let's have any such nonsense, I do implore you. I told you, I'm very satisfied with things as they are. And besides, I loathe executions. I couldn't bear to watch you going through anything of the kind.

JOAN. You have to have courage, that's all; I shall have courage. (*She looks at his pale face and puts a hand on his shoulder.*) You're a good dear fellow, in spite of your gentlemanly poker-face; but there isn't anything you can do: we belong, as you say, to different ways of life. (*She unexpectedly gives him a little kiss on the cheeks, and runs off, calling.*) Soldiers, goddams! Hey there, goddams! Fetch me the clothes I wore to fight in, and when I'm back in my breeches tell all my judges Joan is herself again!

WARWICK *remains alone, wiping his cheek.*

WARWICK. How out of place this all is. What bad form. It's impossible to get on well with these French for long.

A great clamour.

CROWD. Death to the witch! Burn the heretic! Kill her, kill her, kill her!

All the actors return quickly, grasping faggots: the EXECUTIONER dragging JOAN with the help of TWO ENGLISH SOLDIERS. LADVENU follows, very pale. The movement is rapid and brutal. The EXECUTIONER, with someone's help, perhaps the PROMOTER'S, makes

*a stake with the benches from the trial scene. They
make* JOAN *climb up. they tie her to the stake, and
nail a defamatory inscription over her head. The*
CROWD *yells.*

CROWD. To the stake with the witch! To the stake! Shave
her head, the soldier's bitch! To the stake! To the stake!
Burn her!

WARWICK. Stupidity! Absurd stupidity! This is something
we could have done without, perfectly well.

JOAN. A cross! Let me have a cross, a cross to hold: pity
me!

PROMOTER. No, No! No cross for a witch!

JOAN. Give me a cross, a cross to hold, a crucifix!

CAUCHON. Ladvenu! To the parish church! Run, Ladvenu!

LADVENU *runs off.*

PROMOTER (*to the* INQUISITOR). This is most irregular!
Aren't you going to protest, my lord?

INQUISITOR (*staring at* JOAN). With or without a cross, she
has to be silenced, and quickly! Look at her, defying
us. Are we never going to be able to master this flaunting
spirit of man?

JOAN. A cross!

An ENGLISH SOLDIER *has taken two sticks, ties them
together and calls to* JOAN.

SOLDIER. Hold on, wait a bit, my girl: here you are! What
are they talking about, these two priests? They make me
vomit. She's got a right to a cross, like anybody else.

PROMOTER (*rushing forward*). She is a heretic! I forbid
you to give it to her!

SOLDIER (*jostling him off*). You choke yourself.

99

He offers the improvised cross to JOAN, *who clasps it against her, and kisses it.*

PROMOTER (*rushing to* WARWICK). My lord! This man ought to be arrested as a heretic. I insist that you arrest him immediately!

WARWICK. You make me tired, sir. I have eight hundred men like that, each one more heretical than the others. They are what I use to fight the wars with.

INQUISITOR (*to the* EXECUTIONER). Will you hurry and light the fire? Let the smoke cover her quickly, and hide her away out of our sight! (*To* WARWICK.) We must make haste! In five minutes everybody will have swung to her side, they will all be for her!

WARWICK. I'm very much afraid that has already happened.

LADVENU *runs in with a cross.*

PROMOTER (*yelling*). Don't dare to give her the cross, Brother Ladvenu!

CAUCHON. Let him alone, Canon: I order you to let him alone.

PROMOTER. I shall refer this matter to the court of Rome!

CAUCHON. You can refer it to the devil, if you like: for the present moment, the orders to be obeyed here are mine.

All this is rapid, hurly-burly, improvised, like a police operation.

INQUISITOR (*running from one to the other nervously*). We must be quick! We must be quick! We must be quick!

LADVENU (*who has climbed up to the stake*). Courage, Joan. We are all praying for you.

JOAN. Thank you, little brother. But get down: the flames will catch you: you will be burnt as well.

INQUISITOR (*who can't bear it any more, to the* EXECU-TIONER). Well, man, have you done it yet, have you done it?

EXECUTIONER (*climbing down*). Yes, it's done, my lord, it's alight. In two minutes, you'll see, the flames will have reached her.

INQUISITOR (*with a sigh of relief*). At last!

CAUCHON (*falling on his knees*). O God, forgive us!

They all kneel, and start the prayers for the dead. The PROMOTER, *in a fury of hatred, remains standing.*

Get down on your knees, Canon!

The PROMOTER *looks like a cornered animal: he kneels.*

INQUISITOR (*who dare not look, to* LADVENU *who is near him and holding the cross for* JOAN). Is she looking straight in front of her?

LADVENU. Yes, my lord.

INQUISITOR. Without flinching?

LADVENU. Yes, my lord.

INQUISITOR (*almost sorrowfully*). And there is almost a smile on her lips, is there not?

LADVENU. Yes, my lord.

INQUISITOR (*with bowed head, overwhelmed, heavily*). I shall never be able to master him.

LADVENU (*radiant with confidence and joy*). No, my lord!

JOAN (*murmuring, already twisted with pain*). Blessed Michael, Margaret, and Catherine, you were brighter than these flames: let your voices burn me. O Lord Jesus, let them speak to me. Speak to me. In the fields, in the heat of the sun. Noon.

AGNES (*kneeling in a corner with* CHARLES *and the* QUEEN).

101

Poor little Joan. It is monstrous and stupid. Do you think she is suffering already?

CHARLES (*wiping his forehead and looking away*). There is still the agony to come.

> *The murmur of the prayers for the dead drowns the voices. Suddenly* BEAUDRICOURT *bursts on to the stage, breathless from running.*

BEAUDRICOURT. Stop! Stop! Stop!

> *Everyone is startled; a moment of uncertainty.*
>
> (*To* CAUCHON).

This can't be the way it goes! Grant a stay of execution, and let me have time to think! For, as I said to her when she first came to me, I don't think clearly when suddenly put to it. But one thing I do see: we haven't done what we said we'd do. We haven't performed the coronation! We said that we were going to play everything! And we haven't at all. It isn't justice to her. And she has a right to see the coronation performed: it's a part of her story.

CAUCHON (*struck by this*). We did say so, indeed; you are right to remind us. You remember, gentlemen: the whole of her life to go through, was what we said. We were in too great a hurry to bring her to an end. We were committing an injustice!

CHARLES. You see! I knew they would forget my coronation. No one here remembers my coronation. And look what it cost me.

WARWICK. Well, really! The Coronation, now! And at this time of the day, as though their little victory came last. It would be most improper for me to attend any such ceremony; I shall go away. As far as I'm concerned it is all over, and Joan is burnt. His Majesty's Government has obtained its political objective.

He goes.

CAUCHON. Unchain her! Drag away the faggots! Give her the sword and the standard again!

He goes.

Everyone joyously drags down the stake and faggots.

CAUCHON. This man is quite right the real end of Joan's story, the end which will never come to an end, which they will always tell, long after they have forgotten our names or confused them all together: it isn't the painful and miserable end of the cornered animal caught at Rouen: but the lark singing in the open sky. Joan at Rheims in all her glory. The true end of the story is a kind of joy. Joan of Arc: a story which ends happily.

They have quickly set up an altar where the stake was standing. Bells suddenly ring out proudly. A procession forms with CHARLES, JOAN a little behind him, then the QUEENS, LA TREMOUILLE, etc. The procession moves towards the altar. EVERYONE kneels. Only JOAN remains standing, leaning on her standard, smiling upwards, like a statue of her. The ARCHBISHOP puts the crown on CHARLES'S head, Bells, a salute of cannon, a flight of doves, a play of light perhaps, which throws the reflection of the cathedral stained glass across the scene, transforming it. The Curtain falls slowly on this beautiful illustration from a school prize.

Methuen Modern Plays

include work by

Jean Anouilh
John Arden
Margaretta D'Arcy
Peter Barnes
Wolfgang Bauer
Brendan Behan
Edward Bond
Bertolt Brecht
Howard Brenton
Mikhail Bulgakov
Jim Cartwright
Caryl Churchill
Noël Coward
Sarah Daniels
Shelagh Delaney
David Edgar
Rainer Werner Fassbinder
Michael Frayn
Dario Fo
Max Frisch
Simon Gray
Peter Handke
Vaclav Havel
Kaufman & Hart
Barrie Keeffe
Arthur Kopit
Larry Kramer
Franz Xaver Kroetz
Stephen Lowe
John McGrath
David Mamet
David Mercer
Arthur Miller
Tom Murphy
Mtwa, Ngema & Simon
Peter Nichols
Joe Orton
Louise Page
Harold Pinter
Luigi Pirandello
Stephen Poliakoff
David Rudkin
Willy Russell
Jean-Paul Sartre
Wole Soyinka
C.P. Taylor
Theatre Workshop
Peter Whelan
Nigel Williams
Victoria Wood

by the same author

ANTIGONE
BECKET
RING ROUND THE MOON

The Lark

The Lark is perhaps the most interesting of all the dramatic treatments of the St. Joan story. It makes no attempt to explain the mystery of Joan, but simply presents the phenomenon that was Joan, in a play whose original flavour has been brilliantly recreated in this translation by Christopher Fry.

'In my opinion this is the best play about Joan of Arc which the English theatre has seen.'

Harold Hobson, *Sunday Times*

Jean Anouilh was born in Bordeaux in 1910. He came to Paris when he was very young, began to study law, then worked for a time in an advertising agency. Passionately interested in the theatre, he became secretary to Louis Jouvet, the famous actor-manager, in 1931, and his first play was produced during the following year. Since then he has written over thirty plays which have been performed all over the world. Jean Anouilh died in 1987.

The photograph on the front of the cover shows Dorothy Tutin as Joan *and Michael Goodliffe as the* Inquisitor. *It is reproduced by courtesy of Angus McBean. The photograph on the back is of* Jean Anouilh by Jane Bown.